ALSO BY JOEL OSTEEN

Break Out!
Break Out! Journal
Daily Readings from Break Out!
I Declare
I Declare Personal Application Guide
Every Day a Friday
Every Day a Friday Journal
Daily Readings from Every Day a Friday
Fresh Start Study Guide
The Power of I Am
The Power of I Am Study Guide
You Can, You Will
You Can, You Will Journal
Daily Readings from You Can, You Will
Your Best Life Now
Daily Readings from Your Best Life Now
Starting Your Best Life Now
Your Best Life Now Study Guide
Your Best Life Now for Moms
Your Best Life Begins Each Morning
Your Best Life Now Journal

fresh start

THE NEW YOU BEGINS TODAY

JOEL OSTEEN

Faith Words

LARGE PRINT

Literary development and interior design: Koechel Peterson & Associates, Inc., Minneapolis, Minnesota

FaithWords
Hachette Book Group
1290 Avenue of the Americas
New York, NY 10104
www.faithwords.com

Printed in the United States of America

First Edition: December 2015
10 9 8 7 6 5 4 3 2 1

FaithWords is a division of Hachette Book Group, Inc. The FaithWords name and logo are trademarks of Hachette Book Group, Inc.

The Hachette Speakers Bureau provides a wide range of authors for speaking events. To find out more, go to www.hachettespeakersbureau.com or call (866) 376-6591.

The publisher is not responsible for websites (or their content) that are not owned by the publisher.

Library of Congress Control Number: 2015945418

ISBN: 978-1-4555-9152-7 (hardcover)
ISBN: 978-1-4555-3631-3 (large print)

Acknowledgments

My first thanks, as always, goes to God for guiding me through the writing process. Next up, among those I'm grateful for are my friends at Hachette Book Group for their help. Also, I am thankful for the creative insight from our Lakewood Church pastoral staff member Steve Austin.

I am grateful also to my literary agents, Shannon Marven and Jan Miller Rich, at Dupree Miller & Associates, who are once again proved invaluable throughout the entire process. Special thanks to my sister Lisa Comes, Dr. Paul Osteen, and the literary services of Lance Wubbels.

Once again, this book includes many stories shared with me by friends, members of our congregation, and people I've met around the world. I appreciate and acknowledge their contributions and support. Some of those mentioned in the book are people I have not met personally, and, in a few cases, we've changed the names to protect the privacy of individuals. I give honor to all of those to whom honor is due.

As the son of a church leader and a pastor myself, I've listened to countless sermons and presentations, so in some cases I can't remember the exact source of a story. Thanks to all who have touched my life with theirs. My intention in writing this book is to pass on the blessings, and to God be the glory.

Contents

INTRODUCTION

He shall be like a tree

Planted by the rivers of water,

That brings forth its fruit in its season,

Whose leaf also shall not wither;

And whatever he does shall prosper.

PSALM 1:3

Introduction

The best decision of your life was to live your life with God at the center. That was the essential *first step* to living at your full potential. Now the key to experiencing an extraordinary life every day is to *grow* in your relationship with God. Scripture talks about how life with God is like a tree and its branches. When a branch is connected to the tree, it receives nourishment and life. It's able to produce fruit. In the same way, we have to stay connected to God so we can receive His strength and be empowered to accomplish all that He has for us.

In any relationship, growth happens over time. God doesn't expect you to be perfect. He doesn't expect you to know everything. He just wants you to keep moving forward with Him one step at a time. He wants to show you His goodness and be a part of your everyday life. It may feel a little strange at first, but just like any new relationship, the more time you spend with Him, the more comfortable it becomes. That's why I wrote this book—to help you connect with God and learn about His ways!

Today, know that God is bigger than your past, your disappointments, and your problems. You may have made a lot of mistakes, but God can turn those things around. People may have hurt you, but if you'll trust God, He'll restore you. Just stay focused on the new life you have with Him. Think of it like a change in seasons. When winter turns to spring, the old is gone and the new begins. The past may have been cold and dreary. Maybe your dreams have been dormant and covered. But now it's Springtime! Spring symbolizes a fresh start. It's a time for new growth and multiplication!

You may not see all the changes you want right away, but remember, you don't see the fullness of spring instantly either. It takes time for the leaves to grow back and the blossoms unfold. It doesn't happen all at once, and neither do things with God. Just trust that He is at work bringing about good in every area of your life.

As you read these pages, be open to what God will reveal to your heart. In Part One, I provide eight keys to staying connected with Him and living your life in the fullness of His blessings and favor. In Part Two, I'll help you confront what is often the greatest obstacle to staying connected with God—allowing your past to be a barrier between you and the pathway of new beginnings with Him. Then in Part Three, I am excited to provide you with a treasury of insight into the foundation and greatest source of inspiration to your relationship with God—living by the power of God's Word and His promises for your every need.

No matter what is going on in your day-to-day life, keep making time for Him so that your relationship can grow strong and you can walk in the fullness of the blessing He has prepared for you!

*Maybe your dreams
have been dormant
and covered. But
now it's Springtime!
Spring symbolizes a
fresh start. It's a time
for new growth and
multiplication!*

PART ONE

KEYS *to* STAYING CONNECTED *with* GOD

It doesn't matter what your present circumstances look like, today is a brand-new day, and God wants to do a new thing in your life and in your relationship with Him every day. He has placed seeds of greatness within you that are about to spring forth. He wants to give you a fresh, new vision for your life, one that's filled with His blessings and favor in amazing ways. But it's up to you to respond to Him. Here are eight keys to your staying connected with Him that promise to take your life to a whole new level and make all things new in your life!

BE *on the* LOOKOUT *for* GOD'S GOODNESS

Every good gift and every
perfect gift is from above,
and comes down from the
Father of lights.

JAMES 1:17

Be on the Lookout for God's Goodness

Just like the sun radiates heat, God radiates goodness. It's not just what He does; it's who He is. God's very nature is good. It's important that we recognize God's goodness. The Scripture says *every* good gift comes from our Father in Heaven, both large and small.

Too many times, God is working in our lives, showing us favor, protecting us, sending us healing, but we don't recognize His goodness. Don't take things for granted. It wasn't a coincidence that you met your spouse and fell in love. God was directing your steps. It wasn't a lucky break that you got that job. It was God's hand of favor. The fact that your children are strong and healthy is not just good fortune. That's God being good to you. All through the day we should be saying, "Thank You, Lord, for Your goodness. Thank You for my health. Thank You for my spouse. Thank You for the opportunities and good breaks You've given me."

The Scripture says every good gift comes from our Father in Heaven, both large and small.

You need to be on the lookout for God's goodness. Our attitude should be, *I can't wait to see what God is going to do today.* Anything good that happens, be quick to give God the credit. It may be something small. Maybe you suddenly have a good idea. "Lord, thank You for that idea. I know it came from You." You finish a project at work sooner and easier than you expected. "Lord, thank You for Your grace with that project." God is constantly working, showing us His goodness, but too many times we don't recognize it. We're waiting for the big, spectacular things.

Whenever something good happens, I'm going to give God thanks. When I see favor, "Thank

You, Lord." When I'm reminded of something I need to do, "Thank You, Lord." When somebody lets me in on the freeway, "Thank You, Lord." When the temperature drops below 100 in Houston, "Thank You, Lord." When I'm protected, "Thank You, Lord." When I see the breakthrough, "Thank You, Lord." I'm talking about living with an attitude of thankfulness and gratefulness. God blesses a thankful attitude.

When something good happens, you're seeing God. Make sure you thank Him for it. Make sure you give Him the credit. You may not think God is doing anything in your life, but God is constantly showing us His goodness. My question is: Are you recognizing it? Look around this week. Be more aware. Psalm 34:8 says, "Oh, taste and see that the LORD is good." If you're going to taste God's goodness, you have to realize that every good break, every time you were protected, every door that opened, and every advantage you've gotten has been God working in your life. Don't take it for granted.

I heard about this man who was driving around a crowded parking lot trying to get a space, going around and around. He got so frustrated that he finally said, "God, if You'll give

If you're going to taste God's goodness, you have to realize that every good break, every time you were protected, every door that opened, and every advantage you've gotten has been God working in your life.

me a parking spot, I'll go to church every Sunday." Right then, immediately, a car backed out of a space, and as he pulled in, he said, "Never mind, God. I just found one." That's the way we are a lot of times. We forget that every good thing comes from God.

Every one of us can look back and remember times God protected us, spared us from an accident, gave us a promotion, caused us to be at the right place at the right time, or made a way when there seemed to be no way. Don't ever get tired of thanking God for His goodness. Remember your victories. Tell the people around you. Keep bragging on the goodness of God. The more you brag on God's goodness, the more of God's goodness you'll see.

Too many times today instead of remembering our victories we're remembering our defeats, our failures, our disappointments. When we remember what God has done for us, it causes faith to rise in our hearts. We know if God did it for us before, He can certainly do it for us again.

I encourage you to do three things:

1. *Expect* God's goodness. Get up every day looking for God's favor.
2. *Recognize* God's goodness. There are no coincidences, no lucky breaks. It's the goodness of God.
3. Always *thank* God for His goodness. Whenever something good happens, large or small, be quick to thank God for it. Live with an attitude of gratitude and praise.

If you do these things, you'll experience more of God's goodness and favor, and your life will go to a whole new level.

Action Plan

But be doers of the word,
and not hearers only…
JAMES 1:22

1. Get into the habit of thanking God throughout the day for every blessing, big and small.
2. Start a "Blessing Journal" and write down every significant blessing, breakthrough, or promotion God brings your way. When you're tempted to get discouraged, look through the journal and remind yourself of everything God has done in your life.
3. Psalm 9:11 tells us to declare God's good works among the people. Tell others about the good things God does in your life and give Him credit. It will encourage them and strengthen their faith and give glory to God.

KEEP GOD FIRST PLACE *in* YOUR LIFE

[God] is a rewarder of those who diligently seek Him.

HEBREWS 11:6

Keep God First Place in Your Life

The greatest key to living a life filled with God's blessings and favor is to keep God first place in your life. When you put God first place and make it your highest priority to please Him, you can expect to live a blessed, fulfilled life. Scripture states, "God is a rewarder of those who diligently seek Him." Notice who God rewards. Not people who half-heartedly seek Him, only seek Him when they have a problem, or come to church only on special occasions. God rewards people who *diligently* seek Him. Psalm 34:10 adds: "Those who seek the LORD shall not lack any good thing." When you seek God daily with your whole heart, you won't be able to outrun the good things of God.

What's interesting about a reward is that it is put in place before anyone claims it. Right now, there are rewards for certain fugitives who are on the loose. The money is already in a fund waiting for someone to step up and claim it. All they have to do is find the fugitive and the money will be released in that fund. In the same way, God has a reward that has already been put in place. It's just waiting to be released. The only catch is we have to meet the demands of the reward. God makes it so easy: "You don't even have to find Me. If you will just *seek* Me—if you will get up in the morning and thank Me, read My Word, and make an effort to please Me—I will give you the reward."

Jesus said in Matthew 6:33, "Seek *first* the kingdom of God and His righteousness, and all these things shall be added to you." Notice the key: seek *first* the Kingdom. In other words, don't seek the blessing; seek the Blessor. Don't be consumed by things. Don't chase after money, fame, fortune, bigger this, bigger that. Chase after God. If you will seek the Blessor, He promises all these other things will be added unto you.

Not a few things; *all* these things. God is a God of abundance. When you keep Him first place, you won't be able to contain all the good things He will bring across your path. Instead of chasing blessings, blessings will chase you.

Sometimes we get up in the morning and think, *I don't want to read my Bible today. I don't feel like going to church. I'm tired.* But once you develop the habit and see the benefit of how you feel refreshed and restored, make better decisions, and have God's favor, you'll think, *I can't afford not to do this.* You'll realize that spending time with God is vital to living a victorious life.

The last few months of my father's life he was on dialysis. Three times a week for four hours a day he would go to the clinic to have his blood cleansed. There were times he didn't feel like going. He was tired or busy or wanted to do something else. It didn't matter; he went anyway. Why? His life depended on it. It wasn't an option. It was vital. My father loved to travel all over the world, but when he started dialysis, he had to change his plans and rearrange his priorities. He knew how important dialysis was to him.

That's the way we need to value seeking God.

Require it as a vital necessity. When things get busy, the children need you, it's hectic at the office, you've got a thousand things to do, you've got to put your foot down and say, "No, this is not an option. If I'm going to be strong, if I'm going to be my best today, if I'm going to have God's favor, I've got to rearrange my priorities so I can spend time with God."

Don't be consumed by things. Don't chase after money, fame, fortune, bigger this, bigger that. Chase after God.

You may have to get up earlier—before the children need you, before checking your emails, before the phone starts ringing. Take time to invest in your spiritual well-being. We feed our physical body at least three meals a day, but often we feed our spirit just once a week at church. We wonder why we feel burned out, unenthusiastic, and lack favor, wisdom, and creativity. It's because we're not taking time to get filled back up. Just like we feed our physical man, we need to feed our spiritual man. When you invest in your spiritual well-being, it will pay huge dividends in your life.

The Scripture says that in God's presence there

is fullness of joy, fullness of peace, fullness of victory. That's where you're refreshed and restored. Take time at the beginning of each day to sit quietly in His presence, pray, and read your Bible. These days, life can be so busy, hectic, and noisy. But when you get alone with God and put Him first, the rest of your day will go much better. All through the day, meditate on God's promises. Put on some good praise music. If you diligently seek Him, you will reap rich rewards and live the abundant life He has for you.

In God's presence there is fullness of joy, fullness of peace, fullness of victory.

Action Plan

But be doers of the word,
and not hearers only…
JAMES 1:22

1. Try to spend at least the first 30 minutes with God every morning, reading His Word, praying, putting Him first before work or other priorities.
2. Acknowledge God throughout the day, thanking Him for your blessings and seeking His guidance and wisdom.
3. Develop a habit of stopping to pray and seek God's will before making any important decision.

RELEASE NEGATIVE EXPERIENCES

Forgetting those things

which are behind…

I press toward…

PHILIPPIANS 3:13–14

KEY #3

Release Negative Experiences

We all go through disappointments, set-backs, and trials we don't understand. Maybe you prayed for a loved one, but they didn't get well. You stood in faith for a relationship, but it didn't work out. You did your best in your job or business, but things didn't go as you planned. One of the best things you can do is release it. Let it go.

We can't walk in victory and receive all that God has in our future if we don't learn to release negative experiences. When we hold on to those experiences, dwelling on negative thoughts and emotions, wondering why it didn't work out, it opens the door to bitterness, resentment, and self-pity. We start blaming others, ourselves, or even God. We may not understand it. It may not have been fair. But when we give it to God as an act of faith, we allow Him to move in our life and work negative circumstances for our good. Our position should be: "God, I trust You. I know You're in control. Even though it didn't work out my way, You said all things work together for my good. So I believe You still have something good in my future." There is power in letting go.

We can't walk in victory and receive all that God has in our future if we don't learn to release negative experiences.

Maybe you've gone through a disappointment. It wasn't fair. You don't understand it. You could easily be bitter, live with a chip on your shoulder, and give up on your dreams. No, God is at work in your life right now. He is directing your steps. What you thought was a setback is just a setup for a comeback. God is getting you in position to take you to a new level of your destiny. Now you've got to get in agreement with God.

Shake off the self-pity. Shake off the disappointment. Quit thinking that God has let you down and doesn't answer your prayers. No, God has you in the palm of His hand. He is directing you every step of the way.

It may not have been fair, but God is fair. If you will let it go and move forward, God has promised to pay you back for the unfair things that have happened. As long as you're holding on to the old, it's going to keep you from the new.

There are some situations we face for which there is no logical explanation. We have to be big enough to say, "I don't understand why this happened, but I'm okay with not understanding why. I don't have to have all the answers. You are God, and I am not. Your ways are not my ways. And since You are directing my steps, I'm not going to waste another minute trying to figure out everything that happens along the way." That's a very freeing way to live.

If you go through life trying to figure out why something bad happened, why it didn't work out, it's going to cause you to be bitter, frustrated, and confused. It will poison your life. If God wants you to know *why*, He is God and He will tell you. But if He is not revealing it to you, you need

Where you are going is much more important than where you've been. But if you stay focused on the past, you'll get stuck right where you are.

to leave it alone. Some things God doesn't want you to know. It says in Proverbs 25:2 NLT, "It is God's privilege to conceal things." If you're going to trust God, you have to accept that there are going to be unanswered questions. Everything is not going to fit perfectly into our theology, but we can come back to the central theme of who God is. God is good. God is loving. God is kind. God is fair. God is just.

In your car, there is a big windshield in the front and a very small rearview mirror. The reason is because what's in your past is not nearly as important as what's in your future. Where you are going is much more important than where you've been. But if you stay focused on the past, you'll get stuck right where you are.

If one dream has died, dream another dream. Don't let one setback define who you are. Don't let one betrayal, one mistake, one divorce, or one bankruptcy ruin the rest of your life. That is not who you are. That is just another step on the way to your divine destiny. Now let it go and step into the new beginning God has in store. Quit mourning over something you can't change. Don't put a question mark where God has put a period. If God put a period there, don't waste another minute wondering why, trying to figure it out, wallowing in self-pity and defeat. That chapter is over and done.

This is a new day. God has another opportunity in front of you. He has another relationship, another business, another breakthrough, another victory. Move forward into the new.

Action Plan

But be doers of the word,
and not hearers only...
JAMES 1:22

1. Identify anything negative from your past you may be holding on to—pain, bitterness, guilt, failures, etc.—and purposely release it to God in prayer. Let it go and determine in your heart not to think about it anymore.

2. In your heart, forgive anyone who has wronged you, not for their benefit but yours. Unforgiveness is like drinking poison and expecting the other person to die. It only hurts you. Release them and what they did to God. He is more than able to take care of it.

THINK
YOURSELF
to
VICTORY

Fix your thoughts on what is true…honorable… right…pure…lovely… admirable. Think about things that are excellent and worthy of praise.

PHILIPPIANS 4:8 NLT

Think Yourself to Victory

Our mind is like the control center for our life. Every decision we make and action we take begins with a thought. Our thoughts largely determine the direction of our life. If we're going to live a life of victory, we have to think the right thoughts.

Isaiah 26:3 says that if we keep our mind fixed on God, He will keep us in perfect peace. God has given us the way to have perfect peace: Keep our thoughts fixed on Him. We can't go through the day thinking, *I hope my child straightens up. What's going to happen if I get laid off? I might not overcome this illness.* When we dwell on

God has given us the way to have perfect peace: Keep our thoughts fixed on Him.

those kinds of thoughts, we're not going to have peace. Meditating on the problem doesn't make it better; it makes it worse.

We need to pay attention to what we're thinking about. All through the day, we should go around thinking, *God has me in the palm of His hand. All things are going to work together for my good. This problem didn't come to stay; it came to pass. Many are the afflictions of the righteous, but the Lord delivers me out of them all.*

The apostle Paul understood this principle. He said in Acts 26:2, "I think myself happy," or "I consider myself fortunate," to be able to present his legal defense of the Christian faith to King Agrippa. Given the fact that Paul could ultimately end up dying in defense of his faith because of the accusations made by the Jews in Jerusalem against him, many people would think themselves depressed if they were in his shoes. They're so focused on their problems, they think themselves discouraged. They watch so many news reports, they think themselves afraid. The good news is that just as you can think yourself depressed, fearful, or negative, you can think yourself happy. You can think yourself peaceful. You can even think yourself into a better mood.

Don't go through the day thinking about your problems, dwelling on who hurt you. That's going to keep you discouraged. You've got to start thinking yourself happy. All through the day, you should think, *My best days are in front of me. Something big is coming my way. What's meant for my harm, God is going to use to my advantage. My greatest victories are still in my future.*

On purpose, think power thoughts. *I am strong. I am healthy. I am blessed.* When you wake up in the morning and those negative thoughts come—*You don't want to go to work today. You've got so many problems. You've got so much coming against you.*—more than ever you need to kick it into gear. *This is going to be a great day. This is the day the Lord has made. I'm excited about my future. Something good is going to happen to me today.*

Here's a key: Don't ever start the day in neutral. You can't wait to see what kind of day it's going to be; you have to *decide* what kind of day it's going to be. When you first get out of bed in the morning—before you check the news, check the weather, check to see how you feel—you need to set your mind in the right direction. *This is going to be a great day.*

If you don't set your mind, the enemy will set it for you. Very often, the way we start the day will determine what kind of day we're going to have. If you start it negative, discouraged, and complaining, you are setting the tone for a lousy day. You've got to get your mind going in the right direction. Your life will follow your thoughts.

We will never rise higher than our thoughts. That's why our mind is the enemy's number one target. The enemy is called "the accuser of the brethren." He'll try to remind us of all our mistakes, failures, and shortcomings. But just like we have a remote control to change the channels on our television, we need to change the channel of our mind when those condemning, negative thoughts come. When any thought comes in our mind that is contrary to God's Word, we should immediately reject it and replace it with truth from the Word of God. God has put seeds of greatness on the inside of you. He doesn't make anything average or mediocre. But to reach your full potential, your mind has to get into agreement with what He says about you.

I'm asking you to get rid of wrong thoughts that contaminate your thinking and start meditating on what God says about you. If you'll fill your mind with the right thoughts, there won't be any room for the wrong thoughts. When you go around constantly thinking, *I am strong. I am healthy. I am blessed. I've got the favor of God,* then when the negative thoughts come knocking, there will be a "No Vacancy" sign. "Sorry, no room for you." They won't be able to get in.

Remember, you're going to become what you think about. Proverbs 23:7 says that as a man *thinks*, so is he. Get up every morning and set your mind in the right direction. Don't meditate on the problem; meditate on the promises of God's Word. Learn to think yourself happy. Think yourself peaceful. Think yourself victorious. Victory starts in our thinking.

If you will develop this

Remember, you're going to become what you think about. Proverbs 23:7 says that as a man thinks, so is he.

habit of disciplining your mind to think the right thoughts and meditate on what God says, you will have more peace and more of God's favor and victory in every area of your life. And I believe and declare you will overcome every obstacle and become everything God created you to be.

Action Plan

But be doers of the word,
and not hearers only...
JAMES 1:22

1. Study and meditate on the scriptures in Appendix 3 on managing your thought life to get a better understanding of this principle.
2. For the next 30 days, pay special attention to your thoughts. Train yourself to quickly reject thoughts that are negative, fearful, doubtful, or otherwise contrary to the Word of God, and replace them with positive thoughts of faith, victory, and thankfulness.

PROTECT YOUR VISION

Where there is no vision,

the people perish…

PROVERBS 29:18 KJV

KEY #5

Protect Your Vision

We all have vision. Every one of us has a picture in our mind of our self, our family, our future. The question is: What does your picture look like? Do you see yourself rising higher, overcoming obstacles, and living an abundant life? Or do you have a picture of yourself struggling, defeated, addicted, overweight, and never getting good breaks? The pictures you allow in your mind will determine what kind of life you live. You have to protect your vision. If your vision is limited, your life will be limited. Proverbs 23:7 says that as a man thinks, so is he.

Before your dream can come to pass, you have to see yourself accomplishing that dream.

Dare to dream again. Dare to have a big vision for your life, and trust God to bring it to pass.

You've got to get a picture of it. Before you lose the weight or break the addiction, you have to see it happening in your imagination. The pictures you keep in front of you—your vision—not only drops down into your spirit but it gets into your subconscious mind. Once something is in the subconscious, it will pull you toward it like gravity without you even thinking about it.

Many people have negative images in their subconscious mind. They see themselves weak, defeated, inferior, and wonder why it feels like some-

Do you see yourself rising higher, overcoming obstacles, and living an abundant life?

thing is always pulling against them. It's always a struggle. They never feel good about themselves. It's because they have the wrong images. If you will change those pictures and start seeing yourself the way God sees you—blessed, prosperous, healthy, strong, talented, successful—instead of having something pulling against you, it will be pulling for you. You'll be moving toward blessing, favor, promotion, and increase. Our imagination is incredibly powerful. God said of the people who were building the Tower of Babel, "Now nothing will be restrained from them, which they have imagined to do" (Genesis 11:6 KJV). Once you get a picture of something, either good or bad, you're going to move toward it.

Several years ago, a lady came down to the altar for prayer. She had just gone through a painful divorce. Her husband of many years left her for another woman. She was weeping and telling me all the reasons she would never meet anybody, how she was too old and unattractive, on and on, none of which was true. I asked her to do something to help her to get a new vision. I said, "Get a picture frame and put it on the table by your bed with no picture in it, just an empty frame. Every time you look at that frame, imagine a picture of you with the new person God is going to bring into your life."

As an act of faith, she put that picture frame there. Every time she saw it, she would begin to thank God that He was directing her steps, bringing the right person into her life, giving her beauty for her ashes. She got rid of the picture of defeat, being lonely and depressed. She started seeing herself fulfilled and full of joy with the person of her dreams.

Three years later she came back up to the altar. Once again, she was weeping, but this time they were tears of joy. She said the handsome gentleman at her side was the one she saw in her picture frame and that they were going to get married the following weekend.

What's in your picture frame? What do you see when you look into your future? More of the same? "I've reached my limits. My business will never succeed. I'll always be lonely, overweight, addicted." That's going to keep you where you are. You've got to change what's in the frame. You've got to put a new picture in there. Start seeing yourself strong, beautiful, successful, fulfilled. Your life is not going to change until you change the picture.

Proverbs 29:18 says, "Where there is no vision, the people perish." It doesn't say where there is no money, no opportunity, or no talent. What limits us is a lack of vision. Dare to dream again. Dare to have a big vision for your life, and trust

God to bring it to pass. You don't have to figure out how it's going to happen. All you've got to do is believe. One touch of God's favor can bring any dream to pass. But you've got to see it on the inside before it will ever come to pass on the outside.

You may have been through disappointments, but this is a new day. Your greatest victories are still in your future. Get a fresh, new vision of victory for your life, and one day instead of just having a dream, you'll be living the dream. Your vision will become reality.

Action Plan

But be doers of the word,
and not hearers only…
JAMES 1:22

1. Habakkuk 2:2 says, "Write the vision and make it plain." Spend some time over the next week praying about and writing down your vision for your life. Be as specific and detailed as possible. What is your vision for your spiritual life? Relationships? Career? Finances? Health? Other areas of your life? Make sure your vision is big enough that it's going to require God's help to fulfill. It doesn't take faith if you can accomplish it on your own.

2. If you're a visual person, cut some pictures out of magazines that represent your vision for your life. Put them on your refrigerator or in your bathroom. Or use the pictures to make a "life vision" collage to provide an inspiring visual to attach your faith to.

3. If you are battling a serious illness, do like my mom when she had metastatic liver cancer and put around the house pictures of yourself when you were healthy and doing activities you enjoyed. That will help you get a vision of yourself healthy and whole again.

USE *the* POWER *of* "I AM"

From the fruit of his words
a man shall be satisfied
with good…

PROVERBS 12:14 AMP

Use the Power of "I Am"

What follows the two simple words "I am" will determine what kind of life you live. "I am blessed. I am strong. I am healthy." Or, "I am slow. I am unattractive. I am a terrible mother." The "I am"s that are coming out of your mouth will bring either success or failure. All through the day the power of "I am" is at work.

We make a mistake: "I am so clumsy."

We look in the mirror: "I am so old."

We see somebody very talented: "I am so average."

We get caught in traffic: "I am so unlucky."

Many times we use the power of "I am"

against us. We don't realize how it is affecting our future.

Here's the principle. What follows the "I am" will always come looking for you. That's why you have to be careful what follows the "I am." Don't ever say, "I am so unlucky. I never get any good breaks." You're inviting disappointments. "I am so broke. I am so in debt." You are inviting lack.

> *Our attitude should be, "I am approved by Almighty God. I am accepted. I am a masterpiece."*

You need to send out some new invitations. Get up in the morning and invite good things into your life. "I am blessed. I am strong. I am talented. I am disciplined. I am focused. I am prosperous."

What kind of "I am"s are coming out of your mouth? When you have the right "I am"s, you're inviting the goodness of God.

Words have creative power. With your words you can bless or curse your future. Words are like electricity. Used the right way, electricity is very helpful. It provides the power for lights, air conditioning, all kinds of good things. But used the wrong way, electricity can be very dangerous and harm us. It's the same with our words. Proverbs 18:21 says, "Life and death are in the power of the tongue."

Don't use your words to describe your circumstances; use them to *change* your circumstances. Use your words to bless not curse your future. Joel 3:10 says, "Let the weak *say*, 'I am strong.'" Notice that they may be weak, but they're supposed to say, "I am strong." Not, "I am so tired. I am so rundown." That's calling in the wrong things. God tells them to declare what they want, not what their present circumstances are.

Let the poor say, "I am prosperous," not "I am broke."

Let the sick say, "I am healthy, strong, and vibrant."

If you're struggling in your finances, don't go around saying, "Business is so slow. The economy is so down. It's never going to work out."

Jesus said in Mark 11:23, "[You] will have whatever [you] say." That works in the positive or negative. By faith you've got to say, "I am blessed. I am successful. I am surrounded by God's favor."

Perhaps you've allowed what somebody said

about you to hold you back—a coach, a teacher, a parent, an ex-spouse. They've planted these negative seeds of what you cannot do. "You're not smart enough. You're not talented enough. You're not disciplined enough. You're not attractive enough. You'll always make Cs. You'll always be mediocre. You'll always struggle with your weight." No, get rid of those lies. That is not who you are.

What follows the two simple words "I am" will determine what kind of life you live.

You are who God says you are. Psalm 107:2 says, "Let the redeemed of the LORD say so." God wants you to "say so"—to be proactive and declare out of your mouth what His Word says about you. If you don't say so, the enemy will say so, and other people will say so.

People may have tried to push you down and tell you what you can't become. Let that go in one ear and out the other ear. What somebody said about you doesn't determine your destiny; God does. You need to know who you are and who you are not. In other words, "I am not who people say I am; I am who God says I am. I am not the tail; I am the head. I am not a borrower; I am a lender. I am not cursed; I am blessed."

Before anyone could put a curse on you, God put a blessing on you.

Before you were formed in your mother's womb, God knew you and He approved you.

When God made you, He said, "I like that. That's good. Another masterpiece!" He stamped His approval on you.

Other people may try to disapprove you, but don't go around feeling insecure or inferior. Our attitude should be, *I am approved by Almighty God. I am accepted. I am a masterpiece.* When you talk like that, the seeds of greatness God has placed on the inside will begin to spring forth.

Action Plan

But be doers of the word,
and not hearers only…
JAMES 1:22

1. Study and meditate on the scriptures in Appendix 5 on the power of our words to get a better understanding of this spiritual principle.
2. Use the list of positive confessions in Appendix 6 to speak words of faith and victory over your life daily.

BE SELECTIVE *about* WHAT YOU FEED YOURSELF

...the fool feeds on trash.

PROVERBS 15:14 NLT

Be Selective about What You Feed Yourself

Our eyes and ears are the gateway to our soul. What we watch and listen to and who we associate with are constantly feeding us. If you eat junk food all the time—Twinkies, sodas, candy bars—you're not going to be very healthy. In the same way, if you watch things that are unwholesome, listen to things that drag you down, and associate with people who are negative and gossip, you are feeding your inner man junk food. You can't be strong in the Lord and become all God created you to be with a diet like that. You have to be extremely careful about what you take in. You are what you eat.

Today more than ever, we have the opportunity to feed on wrong things. There are over 500 channels on television. We have the Internet, smartphones, magazines, billboards. Every place we turn, there is information trying to influence us. It's not all bad, and there's nothing wrong with being entertained, but you have to stay on guard.

Proverbs 15:14 says that "the fool feeds on trash." Don't fill your mind and spirit with trash. If you put trash in, you're going to get trash out. If you watch programs where people are constantly compromising and being unfaithful in relationships, don't be surprised if you eventually find yourself doing the same. If you're watching people being dishonest, backstabbing, doing whatever they can to get ahead, that's all going into your subconscious mind. Little by little, it's desensitizing you and becoming more and more acceptable. The shock value is wearing off. Before long, you may think, *Hey, that's really no big deal. Everybody's doing it.*

You're going to become what you eat. Take inventory of what you are feeding yourself. What are you watching? What are you listening to? What kind of values is it portraying? Is it wholesome, inspiring you to be better, and building you up? If not, make the necessary changes. Don't feed on trash.

Don't fill your mind and spirit with trash. If you put trash in, you're going to get trash out.

Psalm 1:1 tells us not to sit inactive in the path of the ungodly. If you want to be blessed, you can't sit there passively while people gossip, tell off-color jokes, or murmur and complain. You don't have to try to straighten them out or read the Bible to them, but you should care enough about what you're feeding on to quietly step away. Don't sit inactive. When an unwholesome program or commercial comes on and you feel your internal alarm going off, don't sit inactive. Pick up the remote and change the channel. God's not going to do it for you.

You have to be proactive to guard yourself. Maybe all your friends are going to see a movie, and you don't have a good feeling about it. An alarm is going off in your spirit. Don't just go with the flow and think, *They may get upset. They may not understand. Maybe they'll think I'm old-fashioned and make fun of me.* You have to ask yourself: Are you going to please people or God? Are you going to peck around with the chickens or soar like an eagle? Don't sit inactive.

Several times in Scripture, we are compared to the eagle. Eagles are the most majestic and high soaring of all birds. That's how God sees us. He created us in His image and likeness and put seeds of greatness on the inside of us. Eagles only feed on fresh, living food, while buzzards, vultures, and crows feed on anything, including dead carcasses. The eagle derives its strength from a healthy diet. If we're going to soar like the eagle and be all God created us to be, we have to feed on good things. With modern technology, there are more ways than ever to do that. There are numerous Christian channels and other wholesome options on television. You can listen to good messages on CD in the car, on the Internet, or downloaded free to your iPod. There are so many great Christian books and daily devotionals, and an abundance of good Christian music. It's easy to feed yourself the right food if you set your mind to it.

I read that the average American spends 400 hours a year in their car driving back and forth to work. Many people use that time to feed themselves the wrong things. I like to listen to the news, but I've learned the news doesn't build you up. Once you hear what you need to know, move on and use that time to feed yourself life. Listen to something that's going to help you grow and inspire you to be better.

You are going to become what you eat. Don't feed on trash. Be an eagle. Be disciplined in what you watch and listen to. Make a decision to get rid of anything that's not building you up and helping you grow. If you will be selective in what you feed yourself, you will grow, experience more of God's favor, and I believe and declare you will become everything God created you to be.

Are you going to please people or God? Are you going to peck around with the chickens or soar like an eagle?

Action Plan

But be doers of the word,
and not hearers only...
JAMES 1:22

1. Be quick to change the channel or station when something comes on that is not feeding your mind and spirit the right thing.
2. Don't sit inactive around coworkers and others who gossip, complain, and are negative.
3. Use your drive time and other free time to feed on anointed messages, praise music, and other material that encourages you and strengthens your faith.

DEAL *with* ANYTHING *That* PREVENTS YOUR BEST

...let us lay aside every weight, and the sin which so easily ensnares us...

HEBREWS 12:1

Deal with Anything That Prevents Your Best

If we are going to live a victorious life in Christ, we have to be willing to deal with anything that is keeping us from being our best. It may be an addiction, a bad habit, or a hot temper. Maybe it's not getting to work on time, not treating someone right, or having a critical spirit. God is always dealing with us about something. He is always calling us higher. But anytime we go higher, our flesh has to go lower.

Sometimes we wonder why we feel stuck at the same place, why we can't seem to get out of this rut. It could be because we're not dealing with what God brings to light. When you feel that conviction

> *If you have an area you struggle in—and we all do—don't ignore it, pretend it's not there, or hope it just goes away. You will never conquer what you don't confront.*

on the inside—something says, "You need to treat that person better," "You need to get to work on time," "You need to get help with that bad habit"—those are not just nice thoughts. That is God speaking to you, wanting to bring you up higher. Don't ignore it. Don't sweep it under the rug.

Sometimes we think we're waiting on God when God is really waiting on us to deal with something. It may be difficult, but it's better to make right choices and be uncomfortable for a while than to keep going the same way and miss your destiny.

But many people choose what is comfortable now and then wonder why they don't have victory. It was an eleven-day journey to the Promised Land, but the people of Israel went around the same mountain for forty years and never made it in. They were complainers, negative, ungrateful. God gave them chance after chance, but they kept failing the test. They didn't deal with it and missed out on God's best.

If you have an area you struggle in—and we all do—don't ignore it. Don't pretend it's not there or hope it just goes away. You will never conquer what you don't confront. If you have a problem, get it out in the open. "God, every time I see my friend, she's so talented, she's so beautiful, I tend to get jealous. God, help me." Or, "God, these people really hurt me. I'm having a problem forgiving them. God, I've got this resentment in my heart." When you have a humble attitude, asking God for help in faith, He will never let you down. If you do your part and deal with it, God will do His part and help you overcome.

When God asks us to do something difficult— forgive someone who hurt us, walk away from a friend who is polluting our life, or anything that's a major sacrifice or takes great effort—we can be assured a major blessing will follow our obedience. There is a blessing attached to every act of obedience. If we cooperate with God, there will be a major shift in our life for the better.

You and God are a majority.

I say every day, "God,

search my heart. Am I on the right track? God, show me areas in which I need to improve. What can I do better?" God doesn't require us to be perfect. All He asks is that we keep trying and taking steps to improve. We should treat people better this year than we did last year. We should have more discipline, less bad habits, a better attitude. If you're stuck at the same place, you need to pray, "God, show me what I need to do to improve."

There will always be something that stands between you and your destiny: pride, jealousy, an offense, a bad habit. The enemy will give you the low ground. He doesn't mind you being average or mediocre, not making a difference. But when you determine not to live with things holding you back, deal with issues God brings to your attention, and decide to be all He created you to be, you're going to see God's favor in amazing ways.

I'm asking you to shake off any kind of mediocrity. You have seeds of greatness on the inside. There's no obstacle too big, no addiction too great, no bad habit too strong. You and God are a majority. As you deal with what He brings to light and do your best to walk in obedience, you'll experience God's radical favor, blessings, and miraculous turnarounds.

Action Plan

*But be doers of the word,
and not hearers only…*
JAMES 1:22

1. Spend some time alone with God and pray as David did in Psalm 139:23–24: "Search me, O God, and know my heart…Point out anything in me that offends You, and lead me along the path of everlasting life." Be willing to openly and honestly confront anything He brings to your attention.
2. Be willing to get outside help to overcome any addiction, bad habit, or other issue that is holding you back. Seek counseling, attend some classes, or participate in a recovery program. Be determined to do everything you can in the natural, and God will do what you can't do in the supernatural.
3. Seek out a prayer/accountability partner who can offer prayer, support, and encouragement

when you are dealing with a difficult issue. James 5:16 says, "Confess your sins to each other [not just to God] and pray for each other so that you may be healed." When we bring an issue into the light and confess it to a trusted person, it immediately has less power over us.

PART TWO

SET a NEW STANDARD

When God gave you a fresh start in your life, when He breathed His life into you and made all things new, He did not do it so you could simply feel better for a few days. No, God is in the long-term new life business. But you can't move forward in your new life if you are constantly looking backward and allowing your past to be a barrier between you and your destiny. It's time to let go of past hurts, pains, or failures. Refuse to be counted among the doubters. Trust God to lead you straight through the barriers of your past and onto the pathway of new beginnings with Him!

"I call heaven and earth as witnesses today against you, that I have set before you life and death, blessing and cursing; therefore choose life, that both you and your descendants may live; that you may love the LORD your God, that you may obey His voice, and that you may cling to Him, for He is your life and the length of your days..."

DEUTERONOMY 30:19–20

Take the Challenge to Step into Freedom

We receive our DNA from our parents. The genes passed down determine what we look like, how tall we are, and the color of our hair. People tell us often, for example, that our son, Jonathan, has his mother's eyes and that he looks just like Victoria.

"Thank God," I say.

Not only are physical traits passed down through genes, but also our personality traits, our demeanor, our attitude, and our sense of humor. Our daughter, Alexandra, is very neat and organized. From the time she was a little girl she kept her room perfectly clean, everything in place. Spotless. We never asked her to do that. That trait came from my grandfather. He was the same way. My mother is like that too. It's been passed down for four generations. Somewhere they have a gene that says, "Be neat. Be clean. Be organized. Keep everything perfectly in place."

But just as good characteristics can be passed down, so can negative characteristics. If one of your parents was an alcoholic, there's a ten times greater chance of you becoming an alcoholic.

For years it was thought that there was little anyone could do about bad things passed down genetically. We thought, *Well, too bad. It's in my genes. Depression, addictions, low self-esteem; nothing I can do about it.*

But recently researchers have discovered something they call *epigenetics*, which means "on top of the genes." They realized that the genes passed down to us are not always activated. Their influence on you depends on your decisions, your environment, and your experiences.

Now, while we cannot deactivate what color our hair will be or the shape of our eyes, there are certain genes that we can, in effect, turn on or turn off, the scientists say. They've discovered what the Scripture says: Just because you inherit something doesn't mean you have to pass it down.

You can deactivate the negative genes that have been passed down to you. In other words, just because your mother was depressed doesn't mean you're supposed to be depressed. You may have a natural ten-

When you choose life, you choose blessing, you choose the victory, you and your descendants will see God's favor.

dency toward that. What you have to do is turn off that gene. Deactivate it. Don't pass it down to your children.

It's easy to use genetics as an excuse. "Well, Momma was depressed. Grandmother was negative. Great-grandmother was a complainer. Joel, that's just who I am."

No, that is not who you are. You are a child of the Most High God. And just as you inherited your physical DNA from your earthly parents, you've inherited your spiritual DNA from your heavenly Father. He put in you genes of joy, genes of strength, genes of peace, and genes of victory.

You Can Choose

You may have had a lot of negative baggage passed down to you. In your family line there may be addictions, divorce, depression, or low self-esteem. Don't be passive and just accept it. God has raised you up to put an end to it. You've got to draw a line in the sand and say, "That's it. I'm turning off the depressed gene. I am not going to spend my life discouraged. This is the day the Lord has made. I choose to be happy."

When you make that choice, what are you doing? Deactivating the depressed gene. You're turning it off. Why don't you turn off the negative gene? Turn off the alcoholic gene. Turn off the self-pity gene. This is a new day.

Don't blame the past. Don't blame Momma. Don't blame Granddaddy. Take responsibility and start activating the right genes. If you'll start making the right choices, you can override the negative things you inherited. You can break a generational curse.

You have the power to put an end to it and start a generational blessing. You can pass down things that will make it easier on your loved ones. After all, our children have enough to overcome without carrying around all of our negative baggage.

Even if you don't do it for yourself, do it for your children. Do it to make life easier on those who come after you. The Scripture calls this negative baggage an *iniquity*. These can be passed down for four generations. The things you struggle with, they didn't just happen to show up. Somebody in your family line opened the door.

I talked to a young lady with anorexia. She's skin and bones. Her mother has the same problem. Her grandmother struggled with it as well. That's not a coincidence; it's an iniquity being passed from generation to generation. This iniquity will continue until someone rises up and puts a stop to it. Someone has to deactivate that gene.

God said in Deuteronomy 30, "I set before you life and death, blessing and curses. Choose life so that you and your descendants will live." Notice the warning that your decisions don't just affect you. They affect future generations. No man lives and dies unto himself. We've heard a lot about the generational curse, but what's more important is our generational choice. Every right choice you make helps override the wrong choices of those who've gone before you. When you choose life, you choose blessing, you choose the victory, you and your descendants will see God's favor.

Ernest Hemingway was one of the greatest writers of his day, but depression, alcoholism, and suicide plagued him and his family members. Hemingway took his own life in 1961. His sister committed suicide five years later. His brother committed suicide sixteen years after that. His granddaughter did the same thing in 1996.

It's interesting also that Hemingway's father took his life in 1928. I was wondering what would have happened back in the 1920s if his father had deactivated the suicide gene. What if he had risen up and said, "No. I've been made in the image of Almighty God? I have a purpose and a destiny. I am shaking off these negative, defeated thoughts. I know the power in me is greater than any force coming against me."

If he had taken authority over that negative spirit and instead activated the faith gene, the victory gene, the more than a conqueror gene, he could have changed his family line. He might have broken the generational curse and started a generational blessing.

Your DNA Is Powerful

My questions for you are: Have you settled somewhere way beneath what you know God has put in you? Have you given up on a dream, or let go of a promise, because it didn't happen the first time? Maybe you had a setback. Maybe somebody

Just because you inherit something doesn't mean you have to pass it down.

told you, "You're not talented enough. You're not big enough." But I ask you respectfully, "What are you doing there? You have so much in you. You are full of talent, ideas, creativity, and potential."

When God breathed His life into you, He put a part of Himself in you. You could say you have the DNA of Almighty God. You are destined to do great things, destined to leave your mark on this generation. Your heavenly Father spoke worlds into existence. He flung stars into space. He painted every sunrise. He designed every flower. He made man out of dust and breathed life into him. Now here's the key. He is not just the Creator of the universe. He is not just the all-powerful God. He is your heavenly Father. You have His DNA. Imagine what you can do.

You are equipped. Empowered. Fully loaded. Lacking nothing. Don't you dare settle for second best. Don't get stuck in a rut thinking that you've reached your limits. Draw the line in the sand and say, "That's it. I've let good enough be good enough long enough. Today is a new day. My dream may not have happened the first time I tried for it, or even the fifth time or the thirtieth time, but I'm not settling. I'm stretching my faith, looking for opportunities, taking steps to improve. I'm going to become everything God has created me to be."

Now don't go around thinking, *I could never break this addiction. I could never afford college. I'll never see my family restored.* No, you come from a bloodline of champions. It's in your DNA. That sickness is not permanent. Health and wholeness are in your DNA. You were born to win, born to overcome, born to live in victory. It doesn't matter what your present circumstances look like. That addiction didn't come to stay. Freedom is in your DNA. That family problem, strife, division; it's not going to last forever. Restoration is in your DNA. Lack, struggle, and barely getting by are not your destiny. Abundance, increase, opportunity, and good breaks are in your DNA.

When you do the natural, God will do the supernatural. When you do what you can, God will come and do what you cannot. Don't take the easy way out. Stand strong and fight the good fight of faith.

You Can Choose to Pass Down God's Favor

You may be at the place today where you are dealing with a negative spirit. You could easily settle where you are, let the negative genes get passed down, and make it harder on those coming after you. Or you could make a much better choice and say, "No. Enough is enough. I am not going to live my life addicted, angry, defeated, or depressed. I am not passing down that negative baggage. I'm choosing life. I'm choosing blessings. I'm going to make choices that help my family and do not hinder them."

In the Scripture, God told King Saul to go and destroy the Amalekites, the bitterest enemy of the people of Israel, to totally wipe them out. Saul and his army went out and defeated the Amalekites and King Agag, but they obviously did not complete the conquest, because several years later King David would battle them as well. Agag was the hereditary title of the Amalekite kings.

Fast-forward hundreds of years. Esther is in the palace in Persia. A man by the name of Haman is trying to get rid of her and all of her people. Scripture says that Haman was an Agagite, which seems to denote that he was descended from the royal family of the Amalekites. If Saul had taken care of his enemy when God gave him the power to do it, Esther would not have had a problem with a descendant 500 years later.

Could it be that if you don't put an end to what you're dealing with that your family will still be struggling with it hundreds of years from now? God is saying to you, as He did to Esther, "This is your time. This is your moment. Your destiny is calling out to you."

You can either put up with it and let it conquer you, or you can say, "No. The same power that raised Christ from the dead lives on the inside of me. I will conquer this addiction. I will conquer this depression, this low self-esteem. I will not allow it to linger for future generations to deal with."

That's what my father did. As a child, he was raised with a "poverty mentality." Their family lost everything they owned during the Great Depression. In high school, he was given the Christmas basket donated for the poorest family. All they could afford to drink was something called "Blue John" milk. It was milk with the cream drained off, which gave it a blue tint. On farms it was usually fed only to the hogs. It wasn't meant for people to drink. My father couldn't stand it.

My father was tempted to think: *This is just my lot in life.* Every circumstance said he'd never be successful and never break out of the cycle of poverty. But at seventeen years old, he gave his life to Christ and something rose up inside of him— a faith, a boldness, that said, "My children will never be raised in the poverty and defeat I was raised in." He searched the Scripture to see what God said about him and started seeing himself not as a poor farmer's child with no future but as a child of the Most High God. He rose up and broke the curse of poverty in our family. He took the limits off God and went on to live a blessed, abundant life.

No wonder my dad held up his Bible every

service and said, "This is my Bible. I am what it says I am. I have what it says I have." Do the same today, and you'll be amazed what can happen.

The Surpassing Greatness of God's Favor

What a tragedy it would be to go through life as a child of the King in God's eyes, yet as a lowly pauper in our own eyes. That is precisely what happened to a young man in the Old Testament by the name of Mephibosheth, who was the grandson of King Saul and the son of Jonathan. Jonathan and David were best friends and had actually entered into a covenant relationship. That means whatever one had, it belonged to the other. Moreover, in the covenant relationship, if something were to happen to one of these two men, the remaining "brother" would be obligated to take care of the other's family.

This is your time. This is your moment. Your destiny is calling out to you.

King Saul and Jonathan were killed in battle on the same day, and when word got back to the palace, a servant grabbed

Mephibosheth, Jonathan's little son, picked him up, and fled the city. Going out of Jerusalem in such haste, the servant tripped and fell while carrying the child. Mephibosheth became crippled as a result of the fall. The servant transported Jonathan's son all the way to a city called Lodebar, one of the most poverty-stricken, desolate cities in that entire region. That is where Mephibosheth, grandson of the king, lived almost his entire life.

David succeeded Saul as king, and years later he asked his staff, "Is there anyone left from the house of Saul that I could show kindness to for Jonathan's sake?" He was informed that Jonathan had a son who was still alive, so he ordered that the man be brought to the palace. When Mephibosheth arrived, he was no doubt fearful. After all, his grandfather had chased David throughout the country trying to kill him. Mephibosheth may have felt that David planned to execute him as a threat to the kingdom.

But David said to him, "Don't be afraid. I want to show kindness to you because of your father, Jonathan. I'm going to give you back all the land that once belonged to your grandfather Saul. And from this day forward, you will eat at my table as though you were one of my sons." David treated Mephibosheth as royalty. After all, he was the grandson of the king, and David was in a covenant relationship with his father.

Mephibosheth's life was transformed instantly—that's the good news—but think of all the years he wasted in that dirty city of Lodebar. All the while, he knew he was royalty; beyond that, his father had a covenant relationship with David that gave him the rights to claim what belonged to him through his father. As child of royalty, he should have been bold to claim the privileges of his sonship.

Similarly, you are a child of the Most High God. You were not created to live constantly struggling, angry, and addicted. Those genes may have been passed down, but you have the power to break negative cycles. They may have been in your family for hundreds of years, but when you gave your life to Christ, you became a new creation. He put new spiritual genes in you. You have the DNA of Almighty God.

There is strength in your genes. There is power in your genes. There is freedom in your genes. Now don't settle where you are. Don't say: "Everybody in my family gets divorced. Looks like I'm headed that way." Don't say: "Everybody struggles with these addictions." Or "Everybody has financial problems." Here's the catch: You're not everybody. God has called you to put an end to it. You are equipped, empowered, and well able.

This is what the prophet Ezekiel said in an interesting scripture. "The fathers ate the sour grapes. Now the children's teeth are set on edge. 'As long as I live,' declares the Sovereign Lord, 'you will no longer quote this.'"

They lived by this proverb. Their attitude was, *Since the father had problems, the children will as well. There's nothing we can do about it. Since the father ate the sour grapes, since the parents had addictions, since the grandparents were depressed, the children will struggle in those same areas.*

> *When you gave your life to Christ, you became a new creation. He put new genes in you. You have the DNA of Almighty God.*

That was their philosophy. Then God showed up and said through Ezekiel, "Stop saying that. Why do you keep using your relatives as an excuse? Why do you keep using what your parents did and the way you were raised as reasons to stay where you are? As long as the Sovereign Lord lives, you don't have to be held in bondage by the negative things in your past."

Your parents may have eaten the sour grapes. Your relatives may have made decisions that put you at a disadvantage. But God is saying, "It doesn't have to affect you. It may have held you back temporarily, but this is a new day."

If you deactivate those genes and press forward, all the forces of darkness cannot hold you back. You won't have to eat the sour grapes. You will be redeemed. You won't be under the curse. You will be under the blessing. You will step into a new bloodline.

No matter how you were raised or what has pushed you down or held you back, God is saying, "I created you as the head and not the tail. I made you to lend and not borrow." All it takes is one touch of God's favor. Get in agreement with Him. God has explosive blessings in your future, blessings that can thrust you years ahead.

You Can Live as a Child of the Most High God

I've got some extraordinarily good news for you: There is no defeat in your bloodline. There's no lack, no addictions, no mediocrity. You are a child of the Most High God. I am here to announce that the Sovereign Lord is still alive, still on the throne, and He is your Father.

So you don't have to eat the sour grapes of yesterday. Shake off the self-pity. Don't make excuses. Don't blame the past. Don't blame your parents. Don't blame your circumstances. They may be the reason you are where you are, but that doesn't give you the right to stay there.

Start dealing with the issues holding you back. Start activating the right genes. That's what a good friend of mine did. He was raised in a very dysfunctional home. His father was an alcoholic and would get very violent. As a child, my friend saw his father mistreat his mother, be disrespectful, and go into fits of rage.

Then my friend grew up and ended up just like his father. He was a drug addict and living a very violent, angry life. In his late twenties, he gave his life to Christ and had this major turn-around. Long story short, he became the pastor of a large church and a very well respected man.

He went around the world sharing his story, but he still had an anger problem. Most people didn't know that while God set him free from the addictions, the drugs, and the alcohol, his anger never left. He didn't show it in public, but at home, when only his family was around, the smallest things set him off. Just like his father, he flew into fits of rage and was very abusive to his wife.

My friend didn't like it. He knew it was wrong, but he couldn't control himself. He wanted to get help, but he was too embarrassed. He thought, *I can't tell anybody. I'm the pastor of a church. What would they think about me? I'm supposed to be an example.*

But many people fail to understand that you are not a bad person just because you're dealing with a tough issue. Most likely someone in your family line opened the door. Someone allowed that iniquity and then refused to deal with it. Don't be like them. Don't sweep it under the rug, ignore it, or hope that it will go away. Failing to deal with it will keep you in bondage.

James 5:16 says, "Confess your faults one to another and you will be healed." There are some issues you cannot overcome on your own. You have to swallow your pride and find someone you can trust, someone who will keep what you share confidential—maybe a pastor, a counselor, or a friend. Tell them what you're dealing with. Let them pray with you, stand with you, and bring accountability into your life.

When you get your challenges out in the open and say, "God, I need help with this fault," and take steps to overcome them, that's when the Scripture says, "You will be healed." That's what my friend did. Today, he is one of the kindest, gentlest people you'll ever meet.

What did he do? He broke the generational curse. He chose life so his children won't have to deal with the anger or the addictions. He deactivated that gene. It's still in him. It was passed down, but it's not affecting him.

Refuse to Be the Victim

You are not a victim. You're a victor. You wouldn't have opposition if there were not something amazing in your future. The Scripture says, "When

You are not a bad person just because you're dealing with a tough issue.

darkness overtakes the righteous, light will come bursting in" (Psalm 112:4 TLB). When you don't see a way out, as my friend did not for a long time, and it's dark, you're in prime position for God's favor to come bursting in.

Don't fall into the trap of being negative, complacent, or just taking whatever life brings your way. Set the tone for victory, for success, for new levels. Enlarge your vision. Make room for God to do something new. You haven't touched the surface of what He has in store.

You may be in a difficult situation, but instead of being negative, just dig in your heels and say, "I refuse to live with a negative attitude that I'm stuck with what my family line brought me. I'm not giving up on my dreams. I'm not living without passion or zeal. I may not see a way, but I know God has a way. It may be dark, but I'm expecting the light to come bursting in. I'm setting my mind for victory."

That's what allows God to work. It's not just mind over matter. It's not just having a positive attitude. It's your faith being released. When you believe, it gets God's attention. When you expect your dreams to come to pass, your health restored, and good breaks and divine connections coming your way, the Creator of the universe goes to work.

You may have had a thousand bad breaks, but don't use that as an excuse to be negative. One good break can make up for all the bad breaks. One touch of God's favor can catapult you further than you ever imagined. You may feel like you're getting behind. You're not where you thought you would be in life. Don't worry; God knows how to make up for lost time. He knows how to accelerate things.

Now you've got to do your part. Shake off a negative mentality. Shake off pessimism, discouragement, and self-pity about your past. Get your fire back. Life is passing you by. You don't have time to waste being negative. You have a destiny to fulfill. You have an assignment to accomplish. What's in your future is greater than anything you've seen in your past. We need to get rid of Murphy's Law and live by just the opposite. Your attitude should be: *If anything can go right today, it will go right and happen to me at the best time.*

Nothing will be as difficult as it looks. Nothing will take as long as it seems.

Why? You are highly favored. Almighty God is breathing in your direction. You've been anointed, equipped, and empowered.

You Can Overcome with God's Help

No addiction is too much for you to overcome, no iniquity, no mountain of an obstacle. Nothing passed down to you should keep you from your God-given destiny. The power in you is greater than any power coming against you.

Do not make the mistake my pastor friend made. Do not learn to function in your dysfunction. God didn't create you to have issues or to hide your troubles and feel bad about yourself. He created you to be totally free.

God said He wants to give you new wine. New wine is not sour grapes. It's not being burdened down by the baggage from the past. New wine is fresh grapes, sweet grapes. It's a victorious life.

Maybe, like my friend, you grew up with

unhealthy role models. It's easy for a child to accept the bad behavior of parents and other adults as normal. Maybe your parents didn't show much affection to you, and now you're not showing much affection to your own children. Or maybe there was violence, anger, or disrespect in the home. Don't pass that down.

Deactivate that gene. Be affectionate to your children. I've had fathers tell me: "Joel, I'm a man. I don't hug my son. After all, he's grown."

Let me tell you: A real man still hugs his son. A real man treats his wife with respect and honor. Men, the Scripture says your wife is a reflection of your glory. If she's beaten down, discouraged, and worn out, you're not shining too brightly. She's reflecting your glory.

You need to step it up a notch. Do something to put the spring back in her step, the smile back in her face. Take her to the mall. Buy her something new. Send her some flowers. Write her a note. Tell her how great she is. The brighter she shines the

Choose a better life. Choose honor. Choose respect. Pass that down to future generations.

better you look. That's why I keep Victoria looking fine. She makes me look good!

Another thought: Fathers, your daughter is going to marry somebody just like you. If you treat your wife lousy, don't give her the time of day, and put her down, that's the kind of man to whom your daughter will be attracted. Our children follow our example more than they follow our advice. They're constantly taking everything in. They're like video cameras with legs. They're always in the record mode. They're watching how you treat people, what kind of attitude you have, what kind of demeanor you have. They're constantly watching.

Treat your wife like a queen, give her compliments, encourage her, bring her coffee in bed, open the car door, give her gifts, and make her feel loved, valued, respected, and honored. That way, your daughter will marry a winner. Your daughter will marry a man just like her father.

Now, you may not have seen your father treat your mother well when you were growing up. You may have seen just the opposite. Even so, I believe you can set a new standard. Choose to overcome it. Choose a better life. Choose honor. Choose respect. Pass that down to future generations.

Move the Mountain

We all face mountains in life. It may be a mountain of how you treat your spouse based upon destructive family dynamics learned from your parents, and now it's also impacting your children. Maybe it's a mountain of an addiction, or a mountain in your finances, your health, or your dreams that seems permanent.

When you face a mountain, it's always good to ask God to help you overcome it, but it's not enough to just pray. It's not enough to just believe. It's not enough to just think good thoughts. Here's the key: you have to speak to your mountains. Jesus said in Mark 11:23 (KJV): "Whoever will say to this mountain, be removed, and does not doubt in his heart, he will have whatever he says."

If you are facing a mountain of fear, you need to say, "Fear, I command you to leave. I will not allow you in my life." If you have health problems, instead of begging God to heal you, you need to declare to that sickness, "Sickness, you have no right in my body. I'm a child of the Most High God. You are not welcome here. And I'm not asking you to leave. I'm not saying, 'Pretty please, do me a favor.' No, I'm commanding you to leave my body."

I've learned if you don't talk to your mountains, your mountains will talk to you. All through the day, those negative thoughts will come. They are your mountains talking to you. You can sit back and believe those lies, or you can rise up and declare: "I'm in control here. I will not allow my mountains to talk to me. Mountain, I'm saying to you, 'Be removed. You will not defeat me.'"

It's not a coincidence that God chose a mountain to represent our problems. Mountains are big. Mountains such as generational problems and weaknesses seem permanent, as if they'll be there forever, and that's how they feel. But God says if you speak to the mountains, you will discover they are not permanent.

If you've faced the issue of anger in your relationship with your spouse, depression, or an addiction, it may seem as though it's never going to change, but when you speak words of faith, something happens in the unseen realm. Mountains crumble. The forces of darkness are defeated. The enemy trembles.

When you declare the authority of the Son of the Living God, all the forces of heaven come to attention. The mighty armies of the unseen Most High God will stand behind you. Let me tell you, no power can stand against our God. No marriage problem. No addiction. No fear. No legal trouble. No generational issue. When you speak and you do not doubt, the mountain will be removed.

Now, the mountain may not move overnight. It may look just the same month after month. Don't worry about it. In the unseen realm, things are changing in your favor. When Jesus was walking through a town, he saw a fig tree and went to get something to eat, but the tree didn't have any fruit on it. He looked at the tree and said, "You will not produce fruit anymore."

Notice, Jesus talked to a tree. People of faith talk to their obstacles. Jesus walked away, and it didn't look like anything had happened. The tree was just as green and healthy looking as it was before. I'm sure some of His disciples whispered, "It didn't work. Jesus must have lost His touch, because He told it to die but it didn't die." What they didn't realize was underneath the ground, in the root system, the moment Jesus spoke, all the life was cut off to that tree.

When they came back through the town a little later, the disciples stood there in amazement. They

The power in you is greater than any power coming against you.

saw that tree withered up, totally dead. In the same way, the moment you speak to your mountains, something happens. In the unseen realm, the forces of heaven go to work. God dispatches angels. He fights your battles. He releases favor. He moves the wrong people out of the way, sending healing, sending breakthrough, sending victory.

You may not see what God has done for some time. That mountain may look just as big and permanent and strong as it was before. But if you will stay in faith and just keep speaking to the mountain, declaring it gone, declaring yourself healthy, blessed, and victorious—one day, all of a sudden, you will see that mountain has been removed.

You Can Take Responsibility and Break the Cycle

A few years back we were on a family vacation at a very nice hotel. It was a large place. There were different types of lodging spread all over the property, which was very beautiful. When we first arrived, the bellman took us to our room down this long winding sidewalk. We followed a curving path around bungalows and over this bridge and then around a big lake. I paid close attention because the path to our room was so complicated.

A few nights later, we had dinner at the main lodge. As we were leaving the lobby to return to our room, our son, Jonathan, who was about ten at the time, said, "Dad, you know we're taking the long way. It's much quicker this way."

I replied, "No, Jonathan. I paid close attention. This is the way the bellman took us. This is the right way."

"No, Dad," he persisted. "I'm telling you. There is a quicker way."

"Jonathan, I am positive this is the right way."

For the next couple of days, we always went my way. Each time Jonathan said, "Dad, we're going the long way again."

And each time, I responded, "No, we're not, Jonathan. This is the right way."

On the last day of our weeklong trip, we were again leaving the main lodge to return to our room when Jonathan pled, "Dad, can we go my way at least once?"

"All right," I conceded, "we'll go your way."

Jonathan led us down some stairs through a narrow passageway, and our room was right there! It was probably a hundred yards closer than the way we had been going.

Come to find out, the bellman had taken us the long scenic route so we could see the whole property. I looked at it on a map. We were going in a complete circle, coming all the way back to our room. If I had just listened to Jonathan, we could have gone straight back to our room on that route every day and saved a lot of time.

My point is that sometimes what we've seen modeled growing up is not the best route for our lives.

"My mother was a worrier. Now I'm a worrier."

Can I tell you that's the long way?

"My dad always lost his temper. Like father, like son. I can't control my temper either."

That's the long way, too.

Examine your actions and your life. Ask yourself, "Am I taking the long way? Am I holding on to a grudge and not forgiving someone because that's what I've seen modeled? Am I insecure, feeling less than others because I grew up with people who felt that way? Am I making poor choices, giving in to temptation, and compromising, because that's all I've ever seen?"

That's the long way. Don't get stuck in a rut and go the long way year after year. Recognize what's happening and make the right adjustments.

"Am I taking the long way? Am I holding on to a grudge and not forgiving someone because that's what I've seen modeled?"

A lady once wrote her autobiography in four very short chapters. They went something like this:

Chapter One: "I walked down a new street. There was a deep hole in the sidewalk. I fell into it. It wasn't my fault. It took me a long time, but I finally got out."

Chapter Two: "I walked down the same street. There was a deep hole in the sidewalk. I fell into it. It was my fault. It took me a long time, but I finally got out."

Chapter Three: "I walked down the same

street. There was a deep hole in the sidewalk. I walked around it."

Chapter Four: "I walked down a different street."

Too often we keep repeating the same mistakes, making excuses, and blaming the past or our parents. Take responsibility instead. Don't go down that same path again and again, losing your cool, compromising, being worried and negative.

Break the Cycle

If you break those cycles of repetitive behavior, you will go to a new level of your destiny. If you don't, you'll live a defeated life.

In 1874, a member of the New York prison board noticed there were six people from the same family serving in one of the prisons. He was intrigued and did a study. He traced the family line back to a man by the name of Max Jukes, who was born in 1720. He was known as a troublemaker, a heavy drinker with no integrity. He married a woman just like him. They had six daughters and two sons. Twelve hundred of their descendants were studied. Of those, 310 were homeless, 180 were alcoholics, 161 were drug addicts, 150 were criminals, and 7 of them committed murder.

You can be the one to start a godly heritage for your family line.

Another family that lived around that same time also was studied. The head of this family was Jonathan Edwards, who was born in 1703. He was a famous theologian and the president of Princeton University. He married his wife, Sarah, and was a devoted family man. They remained married for 31 years, until his death. They had 11 children. Fourteen hundred of their descendants were studied. Among them, 13 were college presidents, 66 were professors, 100 were attorneys, 85 were authors of classic books, 32 were state judges, 66 were physicians, and 80 were holders of public office, including 3 governors, 3 U.S. senators, and 1 vice president of the United States.

My point is that what you pass down makes a difference. Your decisions today affect future generations. Like the Jukes, you may have some negative things in your family line. They will continue until someone rises up and puts a stop to it. You can be that person. God raised you for such a time as this. You have the most powerful force in the universe on the inside of you.

Don't be complacent. Don't accept less than God's best. You will never change what you tolerate. You've got to put your foot down and say, "That's it. I'm not going to live my life addicted, angry, depressed, and defeated. I'm deactivating those genes. I'm making choices that help my family and not hinder it."

You can be the one to start a godly heritage for your family line. You can break any generational curse and start a generational blessing. You don't have to eat the sour grapes. The Sovereign Lord is still alive.

Yes, negative genes may have been passed down, but remember, your heavenly Father put new genes in you. In this new bloodline there is strength. There is victory. There is discipline. There is favor. Turn off the negative and turn on what God has put in you.

If you learn to activate the right genes and make choices that honor God, I believe and declare you will break every negative cycle that's held you back. You and your family will rise to a new level of honor, a new level of influence, a new level of favor. You will always live under the blessing and never the curse.

I told how my dad overcame the poorest of the poor upbringings to become the leader of one of the largest churches in America. Certainly, the odds were against him, and not surprisingly, everybody around him tried to discourage him. They said, "John, you're never going to make it out there on your own. You better stay here with us and pick cotton. That's all you know how to do. Stay here where it's safe."

But Daddy wasn't satisfied with where he was in life. He believed that God had more in store for him, and because he was willing to step out in faith, he broke that curse of poverty in our family. Now, my siblings and I, and our children, grandchildren, even our great-grandchildren, can experience more of the goodness of God because of what one man did.

You, too, can affect generations to come with the decisions that you make today. If you're not experiencing God's abundant life, let me challenge you to believe for more. Don't merely sit

back and accept the status quo. Don't simply settle for what your parents had. You can go further
than that. You can do more, have more, be more.
Today, begin looking beyond where you are to
where you want to be.

PART THREE

THE POWER
of GOD'S
WORD

At the beginning of each worship service at Lakewood Church, I have the entire congregation stand up, hold their Bible high in the air, and repeat after me:

This is my Bible.
I am what it says I am.
I have what it says I have.
I can do what it says I can do.
Today, I will be taught the Word of God.
I boldly confess:
  My mind is alert.
  My heart is receptive.
  I will never be the same.

*I am about to receive the incorruptible,
indestructible, ever-living seed of the
Word of God.
I will never be the same.*

This confession of the central role of the Word of God in believers' lives is the driving force in the life of our church and an essential key to you staying connected with God. This is why I asked my editorial team to work with me to put together the following six appendices of helpful information that will enable you to understand the Bible better. If you dare to believe God and just act on His Word, the possibilities for your life are endless!

Beginning Your Walk with God

Jesus came so that we can have a *relationship* with God who is our Heavenly Father. When we accept Jesus as our Savior and Lord, when we are "born again," we begin to have a desire to know our Heavenly Father better. People often ask me, "How do I have a relationship with God?" Let me share some thoughts that I believe will help you.

Make It a Priority to Spend Time Alone with God Every Day

For me, this works best first thing in the morning. I like to spend the first twenty to thirty minutes of my day thanking God for all He has done for me, casting my cares and worries on Him, receiving His peace and joy and strength, and then spending time reading the Bible. Morning may not work best for you. I have friends who spend time alone with God during their lunch break or just before they go to bed at night. Whatever works best for your schedule, make it a priority to spend time alone with God every day.

Read Your Bible Every Day

Find a translation of the Bible that is easy to understand. I like the New International Version or the New King James Version. And then spend a few minutes every day reading the Bible. For the first year of your new walk with God, I suggest reading from the Psalms and Proverbs and from the Gospels. Psalms is a collection of songs and prayers, many written by King David. Proverbs is book of practical wisdom for living everyday life. And the Gospels—Matthew, Mark, Luke, and John—are the record of the life of Jesus. A good plan is to read one chapter from each of these parts of the Bible every day. Before you begin to read, pray and ask God to open your spiritual eyes and ears and make your heart receptive to what He has to say to you from His Word that day. You will be amazed as God reveals Himself to you through His Word.

Spend Time Talking to God throughout the Day

Prayer is simply talking to God from your heart. I always like to begin my prayer time by thanking God for all He has done for me. The Bible says *enter His gates with thanksgiving and praise* (Psalm 100:4). And then ask God for what you need. If you have made mistakes (and we all do!), ask for His mercy and forgiveness, ask for strength, ask for healing, ask for peace, and ask for wisdom and guidance. And then thank Him that He has heard your prayer and He will do what you have asked for. The Bible says,

> *Do not be anxious about anything, but in every situation, by prayer and petition with thanksgiving, present your requests to God. And the peace of God which transcends all understanding, will guard your hearts and your minds in Christ Jesus.*
> *Philippians 4:6–7*

Speak Positive, Faith-Filled Declarations over Your Life

There is creative power in our words. Our words prophesy our future. Every day I like to say what God says about me. Every day I like to make declarations such as:

I am loved.
I am forgiven.
I am blessed.
I am a child of the Most High God.
I am approved by God.
I am in the palm of God's hand.
God is directing my steps.
I am well able to do what God has called me to do.
God is causing all things to work out for my good.
I can do all things through Christ who gives me strength.

Every day and all through the day I would encourage you to make positive, faith-filled declarations over yourself and your family and the situations you face. Don't let negative words come out of your mouth. Don't use your words to *describe* your situation; use your words to *change* your situation. As you do this, you will prophesy your future. And I believe you will see your life and your family and your situations begin to change.

Find a Good Church Home

God wants us to be a part of community of believers. I would encourage you to find a good Bible-based church in your area and make that your home church. Make it a priority to attend that church as often as you can. Get to know the pastor. Listen as God's Word is taught. Serve and support wherever and however you can. As a part of a community of believers, I believe you will continue to grow in your walk with the Lord.

Friends, my prayer is that as you get to know your Heavenly Father and all He has done for you, you will continue to rise higher, defeat every enemy, overcome every obstacle and fulfill every dream and plan He has for your future.

APPENDIX 2

God's Promises for Every Need

ACCEPTANCE

But the LORD said to Samuel, "Do not look at his appearance or at his physical stature, because I have refused him. For the LORD does not see as man sees; for man looks at the outward appearance, but the LORD looks at the heart."

1 SAMUEL 16:7

Know that the LORD, He is God; it is He who has made us, and not we ourselves; we are His people and the sheep of His pasture.

PSALM 100:3

But now, thus says the LORD, who created you, O Jacob, and He who formed you, O Israel: "Fear not, for I have redeemed you; I have called you by your name; you are Mine."

ISAIAH 43:1

The LORD has appeared of old to me, saying: "Yes, I have loved you with an everlasting love; therefore with lovingkindness I have drawn you."

JEREMIAH 31:3

"All that the Father gives Me will come to Me, and the one who comes to Me I will by no means cast out."

JOHN 6:37

For we are His workmanship, created in Christ Jesus for good works, which God prepared beforehand that we should walk in them.

EPHESIANS 2:10

ADDICTIONS

"Call upon Me in the day of trouble; I will deliver you, and you shall glorify Me."

PSALM 50:15

"Is this not the fast that I have chosen: to loose the bonds of wickedness, to undo the heavy burdens, to let the oppressed go free, and that you break every yoke?"

ISAIAH 58:6

"I will give you a new heart and put a new spirit within you; I will take the heart of stone out of your flesh and give you a heart of flesh. I will put My Spirit within you and cause you to walk in My statutes, and you will keep My judgments and do them."

EZEKIEL 36:26–27

"Therefore if the Son makes you free, you shall be free indeed."

JOHN 8:36

There is therefore now no condemnation to those who are in Christ Jesus, who do not walk according to the flesh, but according to the Spirit. For the law of the Spirit of life in Christ Jesus has made me free from the law of sin and death.

ROMANS 8:1–2

No temptation has overtaken you except such as is common to man; but God is faithful, who will not allow you to be tempted beyond what you are able, but with the temptation will also make the way of escape, that you may be able to bear it.

1 CORINTHIANS 10:13

Therefore, if anyone is in Christ, he is a new creation; old things have passed away; behold, all things have become new.

2 CORINTHIANS 5:17

BLESSING

"Worship the LORD your God, and his blessing will be on your food and water. I will take away sickness from among you."

EXODUS 23:25 NIV

All these blessings will come on you and accompany you if you obey the LORD your God.

DEUTERONOMY 28:2 NIV

The LORD blessed the latter part of Job's life more than the former part.

JOB 42:12 NIV

Blessed is the one who does not walk in step with the wicked or stand in the way that sinners take or sit in the company of mockers, but whose delight is in the law of the LORD, and who meditates on his law day and night.

PSALM 1:1–2 NIV

Blessed are those who have regard for the weak; the LORD delivers them in times of trouble. The LORD protects and preserves them—they are counted among the blessed in the land—he does not give them over to the desire of their foes.

PSALM 41:1–2 NIV

"Bring the whole tithe into the storehouse, that there may be food in my house. Test me in this," says the LORD Almighty, "and see if I will not throw open the floodgates of heaven and pour out so much blessing that there will not be room enough to store it."

MALACHI 3:10 NIV

"Blessed are the poor in spirit, for theirs is the kingdom of heaven. Blessed are those who mourn, for they will be comforted. Blessed are the meek, for they will inherit the earth. Blessed are those who hunger and thirst for righteousness, for they will be filled. Blessed are the merciful, for they will be shown mercy. Blessed are the pure in heart, for they will see God. Blessed are the peacemakers, for they will be called children of God. Blessed are those who are persecuted because of righteousness, for theirs is the kingdom of heaven. Blessed are you when people insult you, persecute you and falsely say all kinds of evil against you because of me."

MATTHEW 5:3–11 NIV

COMFORT

"The LORD *himself goes before you and will be with you; he will never leave you nor forsake you. Do not be afraid; do not be discouraged."*

DEUTERONOMY 31:8 NIV

"Have I not commanded you? Be strong and courageous. Do not be afraid; do not be discouraged, for the LORD *your God will be with you wherever you go."*

JOSHUA 1:9 NIV

The LORD *is a refuge for the oppressed, a stronghold in times of trouble.*

PSALM 9:9 NIV

Even though I walk through the darkest valley, I will fear no evil, for you are with me; your rod and your staff, they comfort me.

PSALM 23:4 NIV

The LORD is my light and my salvation—whom shall I fear? The LORD is the stronghold of my life—of whom shall I be afraid?

PSALM 27:1 NIV

God is our refuge and strength, an ever-present help in trouble.

PSALM 46:1 NIV

Give me a sign of your goodness, that my enemies may see it and be put to shame, for you, LORD, have helped me and comforted me.

PSALM 86:17 NIV

May your unfailing love be my comfort, according to your promise to your servant.

PSALM 119:76 NIV

CONFIDENCE

The fruit of that righteousness will be peace; its effect will be quietness and confidence forever.

ISAIAH 32:17 NIV

But blessed is the one who trusts in the LORD, whose confidence is in him.

JEREMIAH 17:7 NIV

For I am convinced that neither death nor life, neither angels nor demons, neither the present nor the future, nor any powers, neither height nor depth, nor anything else in all creation, will be able to separate us from the love of God that is in Christ Jesus our Lord.

ROMANS 8:38–39 NIV

In him and through faith in him we may approach God with freedom and confidence.

EPHESIANS 3:12 NIV

That is why I am suffering as I am. Yet this is no cause for shame, because I know whom I have believed, and am convinced that he is able to guard what I have entrusted to him until that day.

2 TIMOTHY 1:12 NIV

Let us then approach God's throne of grace with confidence, so that we may receive mercy and find grace to help us in our time of need.

HEBREWS 4:16 NIV

This is how love is made complete among us so that we will have confidence on the day of judgment: In this world we are like Jesus.

1 JOHN 4:17 NIV

This is the confidence we have in approaching God: that if we ask anything according to his will, he hears us.

1 JOHN 5:14 NIV

COURAGE

"You shall not be terrified of them; for the LORD your God, the great and awesome God, is among you."

DEUTERONOMY 7:21

"This Book of the Law shall not depart from your mouth, but you shall meditate in it day and night, that you may observe to do according to all that is written in it. For then you will make your way prosperous, and then you will have good success. Have I not commanded you? Be strong and of good courage; do not be afraid, nor be dismayed, for the LORD your God is with you wherever you go."

JOSHUA 1:8–9

Wait on the LORD; be of good courage, and He shall strengthen your heart; wait, I say, on the LORD!

PSALM 27:14

Those who wait on the LORD shall renew their strength; they shall mount up with wings like eagles, they shall run and not be weary, they shall walk and not faint.

ISAIAH 40:31

"Fear not, for I am with you; be not dismayed, for I am your God. I will strengthen you, yes, I will help you, I will uphold you with My righteous right hand."

ISAIAH 41:10

Now when they saw the boldness of Peter and John, and perceived that they were uneducated and untrained men, they marveled. And they realized that they had been with Jesus.

ACTS 4:13

DELIVERANCE

The angel of the LORD encamps all around those who fear Him, and delivers them.

PSALM 34:7

For You have been a shelter for me, a strong tower from the enemy.

PSALM 61:3

He delivers the poor in their affliction, and opens their ears in oppression.

JOB 36:15

"Even to your old age, I am He, and even to gray hairs I will carry you! I have made, and I will bear; even I will carry, and will deliver you."

ISAIAH 46:4

"But I will deliver you in that day," says the LORD, "and you shall not be given into the hand of the men of whom you are afraid. For I will surely deliver you, and you shall not fall by the sword; but your life shall be as a prize to you, because you have put your trust in Me," says the LORD.

JEREMIAH 39:17–18

And He was handed the book of the prophet Isaiah. And when He had opened the book, He found the place where it was written: "The Spirit of the LORD is upon Me, because He has anointed Me to preach the gospel to the poor; He has sent Me to heal the brokenhearted, to proclaim liberty to the captives and recovery of sight to the blind, to set at liberty those who are oppressed; to proclaim the acceptable year of the LORD."

LUKE 4:18–19

For I consider that the sufferings of this present time are not worthy to be compared with the glory which shall be revealed in us.

ROMANS 8:18

Therefore submit to God. Resist the devil and he will flee from you.

JAMES 4:7

Then I heard a loud voice saying in heaven, "Now salvation, and strength, and the kingdom of our God, and the power of His Christ have come, for the accuser of our brethren, who accused them before our God day and night, has been cast down. And they overcame him by the blood of the Lamb and by the word of their testimony, and they did not love their lives to the death."

REVELATION 12:10–11

DEPRESSION

The LORD also will be a refuge for the oppressed, a refuge in times of trouble. And those who know Your name will put their trust in You; for You, LORD, have not forsaken those who seek You.

PSALM 9:9–10

The righteous cry out, and the LORD hears, and delivers them out of all their troubles.

PSALM 34:17

Then they cried out to the LORD in their trouble, and He saved them out of their distresses. He brought them out of darkness and the shadow of death, and broke their chains in pieces. Oh, that men would give thanks to the LORD for His goodness, and for His wonderful works to the children of men! For He has broken the gates of bronze, and cut the bars of iron in two.

PSALM 107:13–16

"When you pass through the waters, I will be with you; and through the rivers, they shall not overflow you. When you walk through the fire, you shall not be burned, nor shall the flame scorch you."

ISAIAH 43:2

"For the mountains shall depart and the hills be removed, but My kindness shall not depart from you, nor shall My covenant of peace be removed," says the LORD, who has mercy on you.

ISAIAH 54:10

For God is not the author of confusion but of peace, as in all the churches of the saints.

1 CORINTHIANS 14:33

Blessed be the God and Father of our Lord Jesus Christ, the Father of mercies and God of all comfort, who comforts us in all our tribulation, that we may be able to comfort those who are in any trouble, with the comfort with which we ourselves are comforted by God.

2 CORINTHIANS 1:2–4

Beloved, do not think it strange concerning the fiery trial which is to try you, as though some strange thing happened to you; but rejoice to the extent that you partake of Christ's sufferings, that when His glory is revealed, you may also be glad with exceeding joy.

1 PETER 4:12–13

ENCOURAGEMENT

God is our refuge and strength, an ever-present help in trouble. Therefore we will not fear, though the earth give way and the mountains fall into the heart of the sea, though its waters roar and foam and the mountains quake with their surging.

PSALM 46:1–3 NIV

Cast your cares on the LORD and he will sustain you; he will never let the righteous be shaken.

PSALM 55:22 NIV

My comfort in my suffering is this: your promise preserves my life.

PSALM 119:50 NIV

*Trust in the L*ORD *with all your heart and lean not on your own understanding; in all your ways submit to him, and he will make your paths straight.*

PROVERBS 3:5–6 NIV

*The name of the L*ORD *is a fortified tower; the righteous run to it and are safe.*

PROVERBS 18:10 NIV

You will keep in perfect peace those whose minds are steadfast, because they trust in you.

ISAIAH 26:3 NIV

"Peace I leave with you; my peace I give you. I do not give to you as the world gives. Do not let your hearts be troubled and do not be afraid."

JOHN 14:27 NIV

"I have told you these things, so that in me you may have peace. In this world you will have trouble. But take heart! I have overcome the world."

JOHN 16:33 NIV

ENDURANCE

Not only so, but we also glory in our sufferings, because we know that suffering produces perseverance.

ROMANS 5:3 NIV

Be joyful in hope, patient in affliction, faithful in prayer.

ROMANS 12:12 NIV

May the God who gives endurance and encouragement give you the same attitude of mind toward each other that Jesus Christ had.

ROMANS 15:5 NIV

No temptation has overtaken you except what is common to mankind. And God is faithful; he will not let you be tempted beyond what you can bear. But when you are tempted, he will also provide a way out so that you can endure it.

1 CORINTHIANS 10:13–14 NIV

... being strengthened with all power according to his glorious might so that you may have great endurance and patience.

COLOSSIANS 1:11 NIV

You need to persevere so that when you have done the will of God, you will receive what he has promised.

HEBREWS 10:36 NIV

... fixing our eyes on Jesus, the pioneer and perfecter of faith. For the joy set before him he endured the cross, scorning its shame, and sat down at the right hand of the throne of God.

HEBREWS 12:2 NIV

Consider it pure joy, my brothers and sisters, whenever you face trials of many kinds, because you know that the testing of your faith produces perseverance.

JAMES 1:2–3 NIV

FAITH

So Jesus said to them, "... I say to you, if you have faith as a mustard seed, you will say to this mountain, 'Move from here to there,' and it will move; and nothing will be impossible for you.'"

MATTHEW 17:20

For in it the righteousness of God is revealed from faith to faith; as it is written, "The just shall live by faith."

ROMANS 1:17

For what does the Scripture say? "Abraham believed God, and it was accounted to him for righteousness."

ROMANS 4:3

Therefore, having been justified by faith, we have peace with God through our Lord Jesus Christ, through whom also we have access by faith into this grace in which we stand, and rejoice in hope of the glory of God.

ROMANS 5:1–2

For by grace you have been saved through faith, and that not of yourselves; it is the gift of God, not of works, lest anyone should boast.

EPHESIANS 2:8–9

Now faith is the substance of things hoped for, the evidence of things not seen.

HEBREWS 11:1

But without faith it is impossible to please Him, for he who comes to God must believe that He is, and that He is a rewarder of those who diligently seek Him.

HEBREWS 11:6

For whatever is born of God overcomes the world. And this is the victory that has overcome the world—our faith. Who is he who overcomes the world, but he who believes that Jesus is the Son of God?

1 JOHN 5:4–5

FEAR

"The LORD will fight for you, and you shall hold your peace."

EXODUS 14:14

"And the LORD, He is the One who goes before you. He will be with you, He will not leave you nor forsake you; do not fear nor be dismayed."

DEUTERONOMY 31:8

"Have I not commanded you? Be strong and of good courage; do not be afraid, nor be dismayed, for the LORD your God is with you wherever you go."

JOSHUA 1:9

Yea, though I walk through the valley of the shadow of death, I will fear no evil; for You are with me; Your rod and Your staff, they comfort me.

PSALM 23:4

The LORD is my light and my salvation; whom shall I fear? The LORD is the strength of my life; of whom shall I be afraid?

PSALM 27:1

"For I, the LORD your God, will hold your right hand, saying to you, 'Fear not, I will help you.'"

ISAIAH 41:13

"When you pass through the waters, I will be with you; and through the rivers, they shall not overflow you. When you walk through the fire, you shall not be burned, nor shall the flame scorch you."

ISAIAH 43:2

"Peace I leave with you, My peace I give to you; not as the world gives do I give to you. Let not your heart be troubled, neither let it be afraid."

JOHN 14:27

FINANCES

"The LORD will open to you His good treasure, the heavens, to give the rain to your land in its season, and to bless all the work of your hand. You shall lend to many nations, but you shall not borrow."

DEUTERONOMY 28:12

The LORD is my shepherd; I shall not want.

PSALM 23:1

He who has a slack hand becomes poor, but the hand of the diligent makes rich.

PROVERBS 10:4

Wealth gained by dishonesty will be diminished, but he who gathers by labor will increase.

PROVERBS 13:11

"Bring all the tithes into the storehouse, that there may be food in My house, and try Me now in this," says the LORD of hosts, "if I will not open for you the windows of heaven and pour out for you such blessing that there will not be room enough to receive it."

MALACHI 3:10

"Therefore do not worry, saying, 'What shall we eat?' or 'What shall we drink?' or 'What shall we wear?' For after all these things the Gentiles seek. For your heavenly Father knows that you need all these things. But seek first the kingdom of God and His righteousness, and all these things shall be added to you."

MATTHEW 6:31–33

"Give, and it will be given to you: good measure, pressed down, shaken together, and running over will be put into your bosom. For with the same measure that you use, it will be measured back to you."

LUKE 6:38

*And my God shall supply all your need
according to His riches in glory by Christ Jesus.*

PHILIPPIANS 4:19

*Beloved, I pray that you may prosper in all
things and be in health, just as your soul
prospers.*

3 JOHN 2

FORGIVENESS

"If My people who are called by My name will humble themselves, and pray and seek My face, and turn from their wicked ways, then I will hear from heaven, and will forgive their sin and heal their land."

2 CHRONICLES 7:14

Blessed is he whose transgression is forgiven, whose sin is covered.

PSALM 32:1

As far as the east is from the west, so far has He removed our transgressions from us.

PSALM 103:12

"I, even I, am He who blots out your transgressions for My own sake; and I will not remember your sins."

ISAIAH 43:25

"For if you forgive men their trespasses, your heavenly Father will also forgive you. But if you do not forgive men their trespasses, neither will your Father forgive your trespasses."

MATTHEW 6:14–15

And be kind to one another, tenderhearted, forgiving one another, even as God in Christ forgave you.

EPHESIANS 4:32

... bearing with one another, and forgiving one another, if anyone has a complaint against another; even as Christ forgave you, so you also must do.

COLOSSIANS 3:13

If we confess our sins, He is faithful and just to forgive us our sins and to cleanse us from all unrighteousness.

1 JOHN 1:9

FREEDOM

I will walk about in freedom, for I have sought out your precepts.

PSALM 119:45 NIV

The Spirit of the Sovereign LORD is on me, because the LORD has anointed me to proclaim good news to the poor. He has sent me to bind up the brokenhearted, to proclaim freedom for the captives and release from darkness for the prisoners.

ISAIAH 61:1 NIV

"So if the Son sets you free, you will be free indeed."

JOHN 8:36 NIV

But now that you have been set free from sin and have become slaves of God, the benefit you reap leads to holiness, and the result is eternal life.

ROMANS 6:22 NIV

Therefore, there is now no condemnation for those who are in Christ Jesus, because through Christ Jesus the law of the Spirit who gives life has set you free from the law of sin and death.

ROMANS 8:1–2 NIV

Now the Lord is the Spirit, and where the Spirit of the Lord is, there is freedom.

2 CORINTHIANS 3:17 NIV

It is for freedom that Christ has set us free. Stand firm, then, and do not let yourselves be burdened again by a yoke of slavery.

GALATIANS 5:1 NIV

In him and through faith in him we may approach God with freedom and confidence.

EPHESIANS 3:12 NIV

FRIENDSHIP

Now when he had finished speaking to Saul, the soul of Jonathan was knit to the soul of David, and Jonathan loved him as his own soul.... Then Jonathan and David made a covenant, because he loved him as his own soul.

1 SAMUEL 18:1–3

He who walks with wise men will be wise, but the companion of fools will be destroyed.

PROVERBS 13:20

A friend loves at all times, and a brother is born for adversity.

PROVERBS 17:17

A man who has friends must himself be friendly, but there is a friend who sticks closer than a brother.

PROVERBS 18:24

"If I then, your Lord and Teacher, have washed your feet, you also ought to wash one another's feet. For I have given you an example, that you should do as I have done to you."

JOHN 13:14–15

"This is My commandment, that you love one another as I have loved you. Greater love has no one than this, than to lay down one's life for his friends."

JOHN 15:12–15

Let nothing be done through selfish ambition or conceit, but in lowliness of mind let each esteem others better than himself. Let each of you look out not only for his own interests, but also for the interests of others.

PHILIPPIANS 2:3–4

And above all things have fervent love for one another, for "love will cover a multitude of sins."

1 PETER 4:8

GOD'S LOVE

The LORD has appeared of old to me, saying:
"Yes, I have loved you with an everlasting love;
therefore with lovingkindness I have drawn you."

JEREMIAH 31:3

"For God so loved the world that He gave His
only begotten Son, that whoever believes in Him
should not perish but have everlasting life."

JOHN 3:16

But God demonstrates His own love toward us,
in that while we were still sinners, Christ died
for us.

ROMANS 5:8

For I am persuaded that neither death nor life,
nor angels nor principalities nor powers, nor
things present nor things to come, nor height nor
depth, nor any other created thing, shall be able
to separate us from the love of God which is in
Christ Jesus our Lord.

ROMANS 8:38–39

But God, who is rich in mercy, because of His great love with which He loved us, even when we were dead in trespasses, made us alive together with Christ (by grace you have been saved), and raised us up together, and made us sit together in the heavenly places in Christ Jesus.

EPHESIANS 2:4–6

God is love. In this the love of God was manifested toward us, that God has sent His only begotten Son into the world, that we might live through Him. In this is love, not that we loved God, but that He loved us and sent His Son to be the propitiation for our sins. Beloved, if God so loved us, we also ought to love one another.

1 JOHN 4:8–11

GRACE

And the Word became flesh and dwelt among us, and we beheld His glory, the glory as of the only begotten of the Father, full of grace and truth.... And of His fullness we have all received, and grace for grace.

JOHN 1:14, 16

Therefore, having been justified by faith, we have peace with God through our Lord Jesus Christ, through whom also we have access by faith into this grace in which we stand, and rejoice in hope of the glory of God.

ROMANS 5:1–2

And God is able to make all grace abound toward you, that you, always having all sufficiency in all things, may have an abundance for every good work.

2 CORINTHIANS 9:8

And He said to me, "My grace is sufficient for you, for My strength is made perfect in weakness."

2 CORINTHIANS 12:9

In Him we have redemption through His blood, the forgiveness of sins, according to the riches of His grace...

EPHESIANS 1:7

For by grace you have been saved through faith, and that not of yourselves; it is the gift of God, not of works, lest anyone should boast.

EPHESIANS 2:8–9

For we do not have a High Priest who cannot sympathize with our weaknesses, but was in all points tempted as we are, yet without sin. Let us therefore come boldly to the throne of grace, that we may obtain mercy and find grace to help in time of need.

HEBREWS 4:15–16

But He gives more grace. Therefore He says: "God resists the proud, but gives grace to the humble."

JAMES 4:6

GRIEF

But God will redeem my soul from the power of the grave, for He shall receive me.

PSALM 49:15

"When you pass through the waters, I will be with you; and through the rivers, they shall not overflow you. When you walk through the fire, you shall not be burned, nor shall the flame scorch you."

ISAIAH 43:2

"Blessed are those who mourn, for they shall be comforted."

MATTHEW 5:4

And Jesus said to him, "Assuredly, I say to you, today you will be with Me in Paradise."

LUKE 23:43

"O Death, where is your sting? O Hades, where is your victory?" The sting of death is sin, and the strength of sin is the law. But thanks be to God, who gives us the victory through our Lord Jesus Christ.

1 CORINTHIANS 15:55–57

Blessed be the God and Father of our Lord Jesus Christ, the Father of mercies and God of all comfort, who comforts us in all our tribulation, that we may be able to comfort those who are in any trouble, with the comfort with which we ourselves are comforted by God.

2 CORINTHIANS 1:3–4

But I do not want you to be ignorant, brethren, concerning those who have fallen asleep, lest you sorrow as others who have no hope. For if we believe that Jesus died and rose again, even so God will bring with Him those who sleep in Jesus.

1 THESSALONIANS 4:13–14

"And God will wipe away every tear from their eyes; there shall be no more death, nor sorrow, nor crying. There shall be no more pain, for the former things have passed away."

REVELATION 21:4

GUIDANCE

"The secret things belong to the LORD our God, but those things which are revealed belong to us and to our children forever, that we may do all the words of this law."

DEUTERONOMY 29:29

Show me Your ways, O LORD; teach me Your paths. Lead me in Your truth and teach me, for You are the God of my salvation; on You I wait all the day.

PSALM 25:4–5

Trust in the LORD with all your heart, and lean not on your own understanding; in all your ways acknowledge Him, and He shall direct your paths.

PROVERBS 3:5–6

"Fear not, for I am with you; be not dismayed, for I am your God. I will strengthen you, yes, I will help you, I will uphold you with My righteous right hand."

ISAIAH 41:10

"I still have many things to say to you, but you cannot bear them now. However, when He, the Spirit of truth, has come, He will guide you into all truth; for He will not speak on His own authority, but whatever He hears He will speak; and He will tell you things to come."

JOHN 16:12–13

For *"who has known the mind of the LORD that he may instruct Him?" But we have the mind of Christ.*

1 CORINTHIANS 2:16

If any of you lacks wisdom, let him ask of God, who gives to all liberally and without reproach, and it will be given to him. But let him ask in faith, with no doubting, for he who doubts is like a wave of the sea driven and tossed by the wind.

JAMES 1:5–6

HEALING

"If you diligently heed the voice of the LORD your God and do what is right in His sight, give ear to His commandments and keep all His statutes, I will put none of the diseases on you which I have brought on the Egyptians. For I am the LORD who heals you."

EXODUS 15:26

Bless the LORD, O my soul, and forget not all His benefits: Who forgives all your iniquities, Who heals all your diseases, Who redeems your life from destruction, Who crowns you with lovingkindness and tender mercies, Who satisfies your mouth with good things, so that your youth is renewed like the eagle's.

PSALM 103:2–5

But He was wounded for our transgressions, He was bruised for our iniquities; the chastisement for our peace was upon Him, and by His stripes we are healed.

ISAIAH 53:5

Then Jesus went about all the cities and villages, teaching in their synagogues, preaching the gospel of the kingdom, and healing every sickness and every disease among the people.

MATTHEW 9:35

And the whole multitude sought to touch Him, for power went out from Him and healed them all.

LUKE 6:19

Is anyone among you suffering? Let him pray. Is anyone cheerful? Let him sing psalms. Is anyone among you sick? Let him call for the elders of the church, and let them pray over him, anointing him with oil in the name of the Lord. And the prayer of faith will save the sick, and the Lord will raise him up.

JAMES 5:13–15

HEALTH

Do not be wise in your own eyes; fear the LORD and depart from evil. It will be health to your flesh, and strength to your bones.

PROVERBS 3:7–8

My son, give attention to my words; incline your ear to my sayings. Do not let them depart from your eyes; keep them in the midst of your heart; for they are life to those who find them, and health to all their flesh.

PROVERBS 4:20–22

Pleasant words are like a honeycomb, sweetness to the soul and health to the bones.

PROVERBS 16:24

But those who wait on the LORD Shall renew their strength; they shall mount up with wings like eagles, they shall run and not be weary, they shall walk and not faint.

ISAIAH 40:31

"For I will restore health to you and heal you of your wounds," says the LORD, "because they called you an outcast saying: 'This is Zion; no one seeks her.'"

JEREMIAH 30:17

Beloved, I pray that you may prosper in all things and be in health, just as your soul prospers.

3 JOHN 2

HOPE

*Why are you cast down, O my soul? And why
are you disquieted within me? Hope in God,
for I shall yet praise Him for the help of His
countenance.*

PSALM 42:5

*For I know the thoughts that I think toward
you, says the LORD, thoughts of peace and not of
evil, to give you a future and a hope.*

JEREMIAH 29:11

*This I recall to my mind, therefore I have
hope. Through the LORD's mercies we are not
consumed, because His compassions fail not.
They are new every morning; great is Your
faithfulness. "The LORD is my portion," says my
soul, "Therefore I hope in Him!"*

LAMENTATIONS 3:21–24

Now hope does not disappoint, because the love of God has been poured out in our hearts by the Holy Spirit who was given to us.

ROMANS 5:5

Now may the God of hope fill you with all joy and peace in believing, that you may abound in hope by the power of the Holy Spirit.

ROMANS 15:13

To them God willed to make known what are the riches of the glory of this mystery among the Gentiles: which is Christ in you, the hope of glory.

COLOSSIANS 1: 27

Now faith is the substance of things hoped for, the evidence of things not seen.

HEBREWS 11:1

INSECURITY

But the LORD said to Samuel, "Do not consider his appearance or his height, for I have rejected him. The LORD does not look at the things people look at. People look at the outward appearance, but the LORD looks at the heart."

1 SAMUEL 16:7 NIV

"So do not worry, saying, 'What shall we eat?' or 'What shall we drink?' or 'What shall we wear?' For the pagans run after all these things, and your heavenly Father knows that you need them. But seek first his kingdom and his righteousness, and all these things will be given to you as well. Therefore do not worry about tomorrow, for tomorrow will worry about itself. Each day has enough trouble of its own."

MATTHEW 6:31–34 NIV

Do not conform to the pattern of this world, but be transformed by the renewing of your mind. Then you will be able to test and approve what God's will is—his good, pleasing and perfect will.

ROMANS 12:2 NIV

Finally, be strong in the Lord and in his mighty power. Put on the full armor of God, so that you can take your stand against the devil's schemes. For our struggle is not against flesh and blood, but against the rulers, against the authorities, against the powers of this dark world and against the spiritual forces of evil in the heavenly realms.

EPHESIANS 6:10–14 NIV

Do not be anxious about anything, but in every situation, by prayer and petition, with thanksgiving, present your requests to God. And the peace of God, which transcends all understanding, will guard your hearts and your minds in Christ Jesus.

PHILIPPIANS 4:6–7 NIV

JOY

Then he said to them, "Go your way, eat the fat, drink the sweet, and send portions to those for whom nothing is prepared; for this day is holy to our Lord. Do not sorrow, for the joy of the LORD is your strength."

NEHEMIAH 8:10

You will show me the path of life; in Your presence is fullness of joy; at Your right hand are pleasures forevermore.

PSALM 16:11

For His anger is but for a moment, His favor is for life; weeping may endure for a night, but joy comes in the morning.

PSALM 30:5

"To console those who mourn in Zion, to give them beauty for ashes, the oil of joy for mourning, the garment of praise for the spirit of heaviness; that they may be called trees of righteousness, the planting of the LORD, that He may be glorified."

ISAIAH 61:3

"These things I have spoken to you, that My joy may remain in you, and that your joy may be full."

JOHN 15:11

But the fruit of the Spirit is love, joy, peace, longsuffering, kindness, goodness, faithfulness, gentleness, self-control. Against such there is no law.

GALATIANS 5:22–25

Rejoice in the Lord always. Again I will say, rejoice!

PHILIPPIANS 4:4

LONELINESS

"Be strong and courageous. Do not be afraid or terrified because of them, for the Lord your God goes with you; he will never leave you nor forsake you."

DEUTERONOMY 31:6 NIV

Turn to me and be gracious to me, for I am lonely and afflicted.

PSALM 25:16 NIV

Though my father and mother forsake me, the Lord will receive me.

PSALM 27:10 NIV

A father to the fatherless, a defender of widows, is God in his holy dwelling. God sets the lonely in families, he leads out the prisoners with singing; but the rebellious live in a sun-scorched land.

PSALM 68:5–6 NIV

One who has unreliable friends soon comes to ruin, but there is a friend who sticks closer than a brother.

PROVERBS 18:24 NIV

"So do not fear, for I am with you; do not be dismayed, for I am your God. I will strengthen you and help you; I will uphold you with my righteous right hand."

ISAIAH 41:10 NIV

"... and teaching them to obey everything I have commanded you. And surely I am with you always, to the very end of the age."

MATTHEW 28:20 NIV

For I am convinced that neither death nor life, neither angels nor demon, neither the present nor the future, nor any powers, neither height nor depth, nor anything else in all creation, will be able to separate us from the love of God that is in Christ Jesus our Lord.

ROMANS 8:38–39 NIV

LOVE

"And now, Israel, what does the LORD your God require of you, but to fear the LORD your God, to walk in all His ways and to love Him, to serve the LORD your God with all your heart and with all your soul..."

DEUTERONOMY 10:12

Jesus said to him, "'You shall love the LORD your God with all your heart, with all your soul, and with all your mind.' This is the first and great commandment. And the second is like it: 'You shall love your neighbor as yourself.'"

MATTHEW 22:37–39

"A new commandment I give to you, that you love one another; as I have loved you, that you also love one another. By this all will know that you are My disciples, if you have love for one another."

JOHN 13:34–35

*For I am persuaded that neither death nor life,
nor angels nor principalities nor powers, nor
things present nor things to come, nor height nor
depth, nor any other created thing, shall be able
to separate us from the love of God which is in
Christ Jesus our Lord.*

ROMANS 8:38–39

*Let love be without hypocrisy. Abhor what
is evil. Cling to what is good. Be kindly
affectionate to one another with brotherly love,
in honor giving preference to one another...*

ROMANS 12:9–10

*Love suffers long and is kind; love does not envy;
love does not parade itself, is not puffed up; does
not behave rudely, does not seek its own, is not
provoked, thinks no evil; does not rejoice in iniquity,
but rejoices in the truth; bears all things, believes all
things, hopes all things, endures all things.*

1 CORINTHIANS 13:4–7

*Beloved, let us love one another, for love is of
God; and everyone who loves is born of God and
knows God.*

1 JOHN 4:7

MARRIAGE

So God created mankind in his own image, in the image of God he created them; male and female he created them. God blessed them and said to them, "Be fruitful and increase in number; fill the earth and subdue it. Rule over the fish in the sea and the birds in the sky and over every living creature that moves on the ground."

GENESIS 1:27–28 NIV

So the LORD God caused the man to fall into a deep sleep; and while he was sleeping, he took one of the man's ribs and then closed up the place with flesh. Then the LORD God made a woman from the rib he had taken out of the man, and he brought her to the man. The man said, "This is now bone of my bones and flesh of my flesh; she shall be called 'woman,' for she was taken out of man." That is why a man leaves his father and mother and is united to his wife, and they become one flesh.

GENESIS 2:21–27 NIV

A wife of noble character who can find? She is worth far more than rubies. Her husband has full confidence in her and lacks nothing of value.

PROVERBS 31:10–11 NIV

"... and said, 'For this reason a man will leave his father and mother and be united to his wife, and the two will become one flesh'? So they are no longer two, but one flesh. Therefore what God has joined together, let no one separate."

MATTHEW 19:5–6 NIV

But since sexual immorality is occurring, each man should have sexual relations with his own wife, and each woman with her own husband. The husband should fulfill his marital duty to his wife, and likewise the wife to her husband. The wife does not have authority over her own body but yields it to her husband. In the same way, the husband does not have authority over his own body but yields it to his wife.

1 CORINTHIANS 7:2–4 NIV

Wives, submit yourselves to your own husbands as you do to the Lord. For the husband is the head of the wife as Christ is the head of the church, his body, of which he is the Savior. Now as the church submits to Christ, so also wives should submit to their husbands in everything. Husbands, love your wives, just as Christ loved the church and gave himself up for her.

EPHESIANS 5:22–25 NIV

PARENTING

"Honor your father and your mother, so that you may live long in the land the LORD your God is giving you."

EXODUS 20:12 NIV

"Each of you must respect your mother and father, and you must observe my Sabbaths. I am the LORD your God."

LEVITICUS 19:3 NIV

"These commandments that I give you today are to be on your hearts. Impress them on your children. Talk about them when you sit at home and when you walk along the road, when you lie down and when you get up. Tie them as symbols on your hands and bind them on your foreheads. Write them on the doorframes of your houses and on your gates."

DEUTERONOMY 6:6–9 NIV

Children are a heritage from the LORD, offspring a reward from him.

PSALM 127:3 NIV

Start children off on the way they should go, and even when they are old they will not turn from it.

PROVERBS 22:6 NIV

Discipline your children, and they will give you peace; they will bring you the delights you desire.

PROVERBS 29:17 NIV

Fathers, do not exasperate your children; instead, bring them up in the training and instruction of the Lord.

EPHESIANS 6:4 NIV

But as for you, continue in what you have learned and have become convinced of, because you know those from whom you learned it, and how from infancy you have known the Holy Scriptures, which are able to make you wise for salvation through faith in Christ Jesus.

2 TIMOTHY 3:14–15 NIV

PATIENCE

Rest in the LORD, *and wait patiently for Him;
do not fret because of him who prospers in his
way, because of the man who brings wicked
schemes to pass.*

PSALM 37:7

I waited patiently for the LORD; *and He inclined
to me, and heard my cry.*

PSALM 40:1

*"For the vision is yet for an appointed time;
but at the end it will speak, and it will not lie.
Though it tarries, wait for it; because it will
surely come, it will not tarry."*

HABAKKUK 2:3

*... rejoicing in hope, patient in tribulation,
continuing steadfastly in prayer.*

ROMANS 12:12

*Therefore do not cast away your confidence,
which has great reward. For you have need of
endurance, so that after you have done the will
of God, you may receive the promise...*

HEBREWS 10:35–36

My brethren, count it all joy when you fall into various trials, knowing that the testing of your faith produces patience. But let patience have its perfect work, that you may be perfect and complete, lacking nothing.

JAMES 1:2–4

Therefore be patient, brethren, until the coming of the Lord. See how the farmer waits for the precious fruit of the earth, waiting patiently for it until it receives the early and latter rain. You also be patient. Establish your hearts, for the coming of the Lord is at hand.

JAMES 5:7–8

PEACE

Great peace have those who love Your law, and nothing causes them to stumble.

PSALM 119:165

You will keep him in perfect peace, whose mind is stayed on You, because he trusts in You.

ISAIAH 26:3

Oh, that you had heeded My commandments! Then your peace would have been like a river, and your righteousness like the waves of the sea.

ISAIAH 48:18

"Come to Me, all you who labor and are heavy laden, and I will give you rest. Take My yoke upon you and learn from Me, for I am gentle and lowly in heart, and you will find rest for your souls."

MATTHEW 11:28–29

"Peace I leave with you, My peace I give to you; not as the world gives do I give to you. Let not your heart be troubled, neither let it be afraid."

JOHN 14:27

"These things I have spoken to you, that in Me you may have peace. In the world you will have tribulation; but be of good cheer, I have overcome the world."

JOHN 16:33

Be anxious for nothing, but in everything by prayer and supplication, with thanksgiving, let your requests be made known to God; and the peace of God, which surpasses all understanding, will guard your hearts and minds through Christ Jesus.

PHILIPPIANS 4:6–7

And let the peace of God rule in your hearts, to which also you were called in one body; and be thankful.

COLOSSIANS 3:15

PERSEVERANCE

He gives power to the weak, and to those who have no might He increases strength. Even the youths shall faint and be weary, and the young men shall utterly fall, but those who wait on the LORD shall renew their strength; they shall mount up with wings like eagles, they shall run and not be weary, they shall walk and not faint.

ISAIAH 40:29–31

"Blessed are those who are persecuted for righteousness' sake, for theirs is the kingdom of heaven. Blessed are you when they revile and persecute you, and say all kinds of evil against you falsely for My sake. Rejoice and be exceedingly glad, for great is your reward in heaven, for so they persecuted the prophets who were before you."

MATTHEW 5:10–12

No temptation has overtaken you except such as is common to man; but God is faithful, who will not allow you to be tempted beyond what you are able, but with the temptation will also make the way of escape, that you may be able to bear it.

1 CORINTHIANS 10:13

For our light affliction, which is but for a moment, is working for us a far more exceeding and eternal weight of glory.

2 CORINTHIANS 4:17

Therefore do not cast away your confidence, which has great reward. For you have need of endurance, so that after you have done the will of God, you may receive the promise.

HEBREWS 10:35–36

PRAYER

"This, then, is how you should pray: 'Our Father in heaven, hallowed be your name, your kingdom come, your will be done, on earth as it is in heaven. Give us today our daily bread. And forgive us our debts, as we also have forgiven our debtors. And lead us not into temptation, but deliver us from the evil one.'"

MATTHEW 6:9–13 NIV

"Therefore I tell you, whatever you ask for in prayer, believe that you have received it, and it will be yours."

MARK 11:24 NIV

And pray in the Spirit on all occasions with all kinds of prayers and requests. With this in mind, be alert and always keep on praying for all the Lord's people.

EPHESIANS 6:18 NIV

. . . pray continually.

1 THESSALONIANS 5:17 NIV

I urge, then, first of all, that petitions, prayers, intercession and thanksgiving be made for all people—for kings and all those in authority, that we may live peaceful and quiet lives in all godliness and holiness.

1 TIMOTHY 2:1–2 NIV

Therefore I want the men everywhere to pray, lifting up holy hands without anger or disputing.

1 TIMOTHY 2:8 NIV

Let us then approach God's throne of grace with confidence, so that we may receive mercy and find grace to help us in our time of need.

HEBREWS 4:16 NIV

Therefore confess your sins to each other and pray for each other so that you may be healed. The prayer of a righteous person is powerful and effective.

JAMES 5:16 NIV

PROTECTION

You are my hiding place; You shall preserve me from trouble; You shall surround me with songs of deliverance.

PSALM 32:7

Many are the afflictions of the righteous, but the LORD delivers him out of them all. He guards all his bones; not one of them is broken.

PSALM 34:19–20

You who love the LORD, hate evil! He preserves the souls of His saints; He delivers them out of the hand of the wicked.

PSALM 97:10

Though I walk in the midst of trouble, You will revive me; You will stretch out Your hand against the wrath of my enemies, and Your right hand will save me.

PSALM 138:7–8

When the whirlwind passes by, the wicked is no more, but the righteous has an everlasting foundation.

PROVERBS 10:25

Every word of God is pure; He is a shield to those who put their trust in Him.

PROVERBS 30:5

Then he said to me, "Do not fear, Daniel, for from the first day that you set your heart to understand, and to humble yourself before your God, your words were heard; and I have come because of your words."

DANIEL 10:12

RENEWAL

Create in me a clean heart, O God, and renew a steadfast spirit within me. Do not cast me away from Your presence, and do not take Your Holy Spirit from me. Restore to me the joy of Your salvation, and uphold me by Your generous Spirit.

PSALM 51:10–12

"Then I will give them one heart, and I will put a new spirit within them, and take the stony heart out of their flesh, and give them a heart of flesh."

EZEKIEL 11:19

Therefore we do not lose heart. Even though our outward man is perishing, yet the inward man is being renewed day by day. For our light affliction, which is but for a moment, is working for us a far more exceeding and eternal weight of glory, while we do not look at the things which are seen, but at the things which are not seen. For the things which are seen are temporary, but the things which are not seen are eternal.

2 CORINTHIANS 4:16–18

Therefore, if anyone is in Christ, he is a new creation; old things have passed away; behold, all things have become new. Now all things are of God, who has reconciled us to Himself through Jesus Christ, and has given us the ministry of reconciliation, that is, that God was in Christ reconciling the world to Himself, not imputing their trespasses to them, and has committed to us the word of reconciliation.

2 CORINTHIANS 5:17–19

SALVATION

"I have blotted out, like a thick cloud, your transgressions, and like a cloud, your sins. Return to Me, for I have redeemed you."

ISAIAH 44:22

That was the true Light which gives light to every man coming into the world.

JOHN 1:9

"For God so loved the world that He gave His only begotten Son, that whoever believes in Him should not perish but have everlasting life."

JOHN 3:16

"He who believes in the Son has everlasting life; and he who does not believe the Son shall not see life, but the wrath of God abides on him."

JOHN 3:36

For the wages of sin is death, but the gift of God is eternal life in Christ Jesus our Lord.

ROMANS 6:23

For I am persuaded that neither death nor life, nor angels nor principalities nor powers, nor things present nor things to come, nor height nor depth, nor any other created thing, shall be able to separate us from the love of God which is in Christ Jesus our Lord.

ROMANS 8:38–39

"Behold, I stand at the door and knock. If anyone hears My voice and opens the door, I will come in to him and dine with him, and he with Me."

REVELATION 3:20

SERVING

"... and whoever wants to be first must be your slave—just as the Son of Man did not come to be served, but to serve, and to give his life as a ransom for many."

MATTHEW 20:27–28 NIV

"The greatest among you will be your servant."

MATTHEW 23:11 NIV

"Whoever serves me must follow me; and where I am, my servant also will be. My Father will honor the one who serves me."

JOHN 12:26 NIV

But now, by dying to what once bound us, we have been released from the law so that we serve in the new way of the Spirit, and not in the old way of the written code.

ROMANS 7:6 NIV

Therefore, I urge you, brothers and sisters, in view of God's mercy, to offer your bodies as a living sacrifice, holy and pleasing to God—this is your true and proper worship.

ROMANS 12:1 NIV

Never be lacking in zeal, but keep your spiritual fervor, serving the Lord.

ROMANS 12:11 NIV

You, my brothers and sisters, were called to be free. But do not use your freedom to indulge the flesh; rather, serve one another humbly in love.

GALATIANS 5:13 NIV

Each of you should use whatever gift you have received to serve others, as faithful stewards of God's grace in its various forms.

1 PETER 4:10 NIV

SPIRITUAL POWER

God, You are more awesome than Your holy places. The God of Israel is He who gives strength and power to His people. Blessed be God!

PSALM 68:35

"But you shall receive power when the Holy Spirit has come upon you; and you shall be witnesses to Me in Jerusalem, and in all Judea and Samaria, and to the end of the earth."

ACTS 1:8

And when they had prayed, the place where they were assembled together was shaken; and they were all filled with the Holy Spirit, and they spoke the word of God with boldness.

ACTS 4:31

For sin shall not have dominion over you, for you are not under law but under grace.

ROMANS 6:14

Now to Him who is able to do exceedingly abundantly above all that we ask or think, according to the power that works in us, to Him be glory in the church by Christ Jesus to all generations, forever and ever. Amen.

EPHESIANS 3:20–21

Finally, my brethren, be strong in the Lord and in the power of His might. Put on the whole armor of God, that you may be able to stand against the wiles of the devil.

EPHESIANS 6:10–11

. . . . that I may know Him and the power of His resurrection, and the fellowship of His sufferings, being conformed to His death.

PHILIPPIANS 3:10

I can do all things through Christ who strengthens me.

PHILIPPIANS 4:13

STRENGTH

"The L<small>ORD</small> is my strength and song, and He has become my salvation; He is my God, and I will praise Him; my father's God, and I will exalt Him."

E<small>XODUS</small> 15:2

The L<small>ORD</small> is my light and my salvation; whom shall I fear? The L<small>ORD</small> is the strength of my life; of whom shall I be afraid?

P<small>SALM</small> 27:1

Be of good courage, and He shall strengthen your heart, all you who hope in the L<small>ORD</small>.

P<small>SALM</small> 31:24

He gives power to the weak, and to those who have no might He increases strength. Even the youths shall faint and be weary, and the young men shall utterly fall, but those who wait on the L<small>ORD</small> shall renew their strength; they shall mount up with wings like eagles, they shall run and not be weary, they shall walk and not faint.

I<small>SAIAH</small> 40:29–31

"Fear not, for I am with you; be not dismayed, for I am your God. I will strengthen you, yes, I will help you, I will uphold you with My righteous right hand."

ISAIAH 41:10

And He said to me, "My grace is sufficient for you, for My strength is made perfect in weakness."

2 CORINTHIANS 12:9

I can do all things through Christ who strengthens me.

PHILIPPIANS 4:13

STRESS

"Have I not commanded you? Be strong and courageous. Do not be afraid; do not be discouraged, for the LORD your God will be with you wherever you go."

JOSHUA 1:9 NIV

Cast your cares on the LORD and he will sustain you; he will never let the righteous be shaken.

PSALM 55:22 NIV

"But blessed is the one who trusts in the LORD, whose confidence is in him. They will be like a tree planted by the water that sends out its roots by the stream. It does not fear when heat comes; its leaves are always green. It has no worries in a year of drought and never fails to bear fruit."

JEREMIAH 17:7–8 NIV

"Come to me, all you who are weary and burdened, and I will give you rest. Take my yoke upon you and learn from me, for I am gentle and humble in heart, and you will find rest for your souls. For my yoke is easy and my burden is light."

MATTHEW 11:28–30 NIV

We are hard pressed on every side, but not crushed; perplexed, but not in despair; persecuted, but not abandoned; struck down, but not destroyed.

2 CORINTHIANS 4:8–9 NIV

For though we live in the world, we do not wage war as the world does. The weapons we fight with are not the weapons of the world. On the contrary, they have divine power to demolish strongholds. We demolish arguments and every pretension that sets itself up against the knowledge of God, and we take captive every thought to make it obedient to Christ.

2 CORINTHIANS 10:3–5 NIV

Do not be anxious about anything, but in every situation, by prayer and petition, with thanksgiving, present your requests to God. And the peace of God, which transcends all understanding, will guard your hearts and your minds in Christ Jesus.

PHILIPPIANS 4:6–7 NIV

Humble yourselves, therefore, under God's mighty hand, that he may lift you up in due time. Cast all your anxiety on him because he cares for you.

1 PETER 5:6–7 NIV

UNITY

How good and pleasant it is when God's people live together in unity!

PSALM 133:1 NIV

"I in them and you in me—so that they may be brought to complete unity. Then the world will know that you sent me and have loved them even as you have loved me."

JOHN 17:23 NIV

I appeal to you, brothers and sisters, in the name of our Lord Jesus Christ, that all of you agree with one another in what you say and that there be no divisions among you, but that you be perfectly united in mind and thought.

1 CORINTHIANS 1:10 NIV

Just as a body, though one, has many parts, but all its many parts form one body, so it is with Christ. For we were all baptized by one Spirit so as to form one body—whether Jews or Gentiles, slave or free—and we were all given the one Spirit to drink.

1 CORINTHIANS 12:12–13 NIV

There is neither Jew nor Gentile, neither slave nor free, nor is there male and female, for you are all one in Christ Jesus.

GALATIANS 3:26–28 NIV

For he himself is our peace, who has made the two groups one and has destroyed the barrier, the dividing wall of hostility.

EPHESIANS 2:14 NIV

Make every effort to keep the unity of the Spirit through the bond of peace.

EPHESIANS 4:3 NIV

And over all these virtues put on love, which binds them all together in perfect unity.

COLOSSIANS 3:14 NIV

VICTORY

"For the LORD your God is the one who goes with you to fight for you against your enemies to give you victory."

DEUTERONOMY 20:4 NIV

From the LORD comes deliverance. May your blessing be on your people.

PSALM 3:8 NIV

"I have told you these things, so that in me you may have peace. In this world you will have trouble. But take heart! I have overcome the world."

JOHN 16:33 NIV

What, then, shall we say in response to these things? If God is for us, who can be against us?

ROMANS 8:31 NIV

No temptation has overtaken you except what is common to mankind. And God is faithful; he will not let you be tempted beyond what you can bear. But when you are tempted, he will also provide a way out so that you can endure it.

1 CORINTHIANS 10:13 NIV

"Where, O death, is your victory? Where, O death, is your sting?"

1 CORINTHIANS 15:55 NIV

But thanks be to God! He gives us the victory through our Lord Jesus Christ.

1 CORINTHIANS 15:57 NIV

. . . for everyone born of God overcomes the world. This is the victory that has overcome the world, even our faith.

1 JOHN 5:4 NIV

APPENDIX 3

Scriptures on Managing Our Thought Life

1. "For as he thinks in his heart, so is he."—Proverbs 23:7

   COMMENT: This verse tells us that *we become what we think about.* Our life will follow our most dominant thoughts. It's like the saying: "Whether you think you can or think you can't, you're right." Ten out of the twelve spies Moses sent to spy out the Promised Land came back saying, "There are giants in the land, and we are like grasshoppers compared to them" (Numbers 13:33, paraphrased). They didn't see themselves as able, and none of them entered into the Promised Land. But two spies, Joshua and Caleb said, "Let us go up at once and take possession, for we are well able to overcome it" (Numbers 13:30). They were the only two people from that generation of Israelites to enter the Promised Land. Do you see yourself as well able to do what God has called you to do, or do you see yourself as a grasshopper?

2. "Finally, brethren, whatever is true, whatever is honorable, whatever is right, whatever is pure, whatever is lovely, whatever is of good repute, if there is *any* excellence and if *anything* worthy of praise, *dwell* on these things."—Philippians 4:8 NASB, emphasis added

COMMENT: This verse tells us to dwell on what is good in our life, not what's wrong. Dwell on God and His truth, not our problems. Dwell on positive, faith-filled thoughts. We are the only ones who can manage our thought life; God is not going to do it for us.

We have to choose to dwell on thoughts that are going to lead to victory, not defeat.

3. "And do not be conformed to this world, but be transformed by the renewing of your mind…"—Romans 12:2

COMMENT: This verse tells us not to think and act like the world, and it tells us how to be transformed—by renewing our mind. How do we renew our mind? By filling it daily with the Word of God, praise music, anointed messages, and positive confessions.

4. "And be constantly renewed in the spirit of your mind [having a fresh mental and spiritual attitude]."—Ephesians 4:23 AMP

COMMENT: This verse tells us that renewing our mind is not a once-in-the-morning thing, but something we have to do "constantly" all throughout the day.

5. "…we take captive every thought to make it obedient to Christ."—2 Corinthians 10:5 NIV

COMMENT: Like the previous verse that talked about "constantly" renewing our mind, this verse tells us to take every single thought "captive" to make it obedient to Christ. God is telling us to manage our thought life so that every thought lines up with His Word. When a thought comes in that doesn't line up with His Word, we need to be proactive to reject it and replace it with thoughts that do.

6. "You will keep him in perfect peace, whose mind is stayed on You."—Isaiah 26:3

COMMENT: This verse tells us how to stay in perfect peace, no matter what's going on in our life: Keep our mind *stayed* on God—not our problems, what's going on in the economy and world, or what people are saying and doing. If we'll do that, He promises to keep us in not just peace, but *perfect* peace.

7. "Set your mind on things above, not on things on the earth."—Colossians 3:2

COMMENT: Like the previous verse that tells us to keep our mind stayed on God, this one tells us to *set* our mind on things above, not what's going on in this earthly plane. The key word is *set*. We have to set our minds on things above; God is not going to set it for us. And if we don't set it, the enemy will set it, our emotions will set it, our circumstances will set it, and other people will set it. We have to actively set our mind on the right things all day long.

APPENDIX 4

One-Year Bible Reading Plan

To help you begin your journey to becoming the best version of you and getting to know and understand God better, this one-year Bible reading plan will provide you with nourishment through every stage of your Christian development.

JANUARY

1   Gen. 1–2; Matt. 1
2   Gen. 3–5; Matt. 2
3   Gen. 6–8; Matt. 3
4   Gen. 9–11; Matt. 4
5   Gen. 12–14; Matt. 5:1-26
6   Gen. 15–17; Matt. 5:27-48
7   Gen. 18–19; Matt. 6
8   Gen. 20–22; Matt. 7
9   Gen. 23–24; Matt. 8
10   Gen. 25–26; Matt. 9:1-17
11   Gen. 27–28; Matt. 9:18-38
12   Gen. 29–30; Matt. 10:1-23
13   Gen. 31–32; Matt. 10:24-42
14   Gen. 33–35; Matt. 11
15   Gen. 36–37; Matt. 12:1-21
16   Gen. 38–40; Matt. 12:22-50
17   Gen. 41; Matt. 13:1-32
18   Gen. 42–43; Matt. 13:33-58
19   Gen. 44–45; Matt. 14:1-21
20   Gen. 46–48; Matt. 14:22-36
21   Gen. 49–50; Matt. 15:1-20
22   Ex. 1–3; Matt. 15:21-39
23   Ex. 4–6; Matt. 16
24   Ex. 7–8; Matt. 17
25   Ex. 9–10; Matt. 18:1-20
26   Ex. 11–12; Matt. 18:21-35
27   Ex. 13–15; Matt. 19:1-15
28   Ex. 16–18; Matt. 19:16-30
29   Ex. 19–21; Matt. 20:1-16
30   Ex. 22–24; Matt. 20:17-34
31. Ex. 25–26; Matt. 21:1-22

FEBRUARY

1   Ex. 27–28; Matt. 21:23-46
2   Ex. 29–30; Matt. 22:1-22
3   Ex. 31–33; Matt. 22:23-46
4   Ex. 34–36; Matt. 23:1-22
5   Ex. 37–38; Matt. 23:23-39
6   Ex. 39–40; Matt. 24:1-22
7   Lev. 1–3; Matt. 24:23-51
8   Lev. 4–6; Matt. 25:1-30
9   Lev. 7–9; Matt. 25:31-46
10   Lev. 10–12; Matt. 26:1-19
11   Lev. 13; Matt. 26:20-54
12   Lev. 14; Matt. 26:55-75
13   Lev. 15–17; Matt. 27:1-31
14   Lev. 18–19; Matt. 27:32-66
15   Lev. 20–21; Matt. 28
16   Lev. 22–23; Mark 1:1-22
17   Lev. 24–25; Mark 1:23-45
18   Lev. 26–27; Mark 2
19   Num. 1–2; Mark 3:1-21
20   Num. 3–4; Mark 3:22-35
21   Num. 5–6; Mark 4:1-20
22   Num. 7; Mark 4:21-41
23   Num. 8–10; Mark 5:1-20
24   Num. 11–13; Mark 5:21-43
25   Num. 14–15; Mark 6:1-32
26   Num. 16–17; Mark 6:33-56

27 Num. 18–20; Mark 7:1-13

28 Num. 21–22; Mark 7:14-37

29 Num. 23–25; Mark 8:1-21

MARCH

1   Num. 26–27; Mark 8:22-38

2   Num. 28–29; Mark 9:1-29

3   Num. 30–31; Mark 9:30-50

4   Num. 32–33; Mark 10:1-31

5   Num. 34–36; Mark 10:32-52

6   Deut. 1–2; Mark 11:1-19

7   Deut. 3–4; Mark 11:20-33

8   Deut. 5–7; Mark 12:1-27

9   Deut. 8–10; Mark 12:28-44

10 Deut. 11–13; Mark 13:1-13

11 Deut. 14–16; Mark 13:14-37

12 Deut. 17–19; Mark 14:1-25

13 Deut. 20–22; Mark 14:26-50

14 Deut. 23–25; Mark 14:51-72

15 Deut. 26–27; Mark 15:1-26

16 Deut. 28; Mark 15:27-47

17 Deut. 29–30; Mark 16

18 Deut. 31–32; Luke 1:1-23

19 Deut. 33–34; Luke 1:24-56

20 Josh. 1–3; Luke 1:57-80

21 Josh. 4–6; Luke 2:1-24

22 Josh. 7–8; Luke 2:25-52

23 Josh. 9–10; Luke 3

24 Josh. 11–13; Luke 4:1-32

25 Josh. 14–15; Luke 4:33-44

26 Josh. 16–18; Luke 5:1-16

27 Josh. 19–20; Luke 5:17-39

28 Josh. 21–22; Luke 6:1-26

29 Josh. 23–24; Luke 6:27-49

30 Judg. 1–2; Luke 7:1-30

31. Judg. 3–5; Luke 7:31-50

APRIL

1   Judg. 6–7; Luke 8:1-21

2   Judg. 8–9; Luke 8:22-56

3   Judg. 10–11; Luke 9:1-36

4   Judg. 12–14; Luke 9:37-62

5   Judg. 15–17; Luke 10:1-24

6   Judg. 18–19; Luke 10:25-42

7   Judg. 20–21; Luke 11:1-28

8   Ruth; Luke 11:29-54

9   1 Sam. 1–3; Luke 12:1-34

10 1 Sam. 4–6; Luke 12:35-59

11 1 Sam. 7–9; Luke 13:1-21

12 1 Sam. 10–12; Luke 13:22-35

13 1 Sam. 13–14; Luke 14:1-24

14 1 Sam. 15–16; Luke 14:25-35

15 1 Sam. 17–18; Luke 15:1-10

16 1 Sam. 19–21; Luke 15:11-32

17 1 Sam. 22–24; Luke 16:1-18

18 1 Sam. 25–26; Luke 16:19-31

19 1 Sam. 27–29; Luke 17:1-19

20 1 Sam. 30–31; Luke 17:20-37

21 2 Sam. 1–3; Luke 18:1-17

22 2 Sam. 4–6; Luke 18:18-43

23 2 Sam. 7–9; Luke 19:1-28

24 2 Sam. 10–12; Luke 19:29-48

25 2 Sam. 13–14; Luke 20:1-26

26 2 Sam. 15–16; Luke 20:27-47

27 2 Sam. 17–18; Luke 21:1-19

28 2 Sam. 19–20; Luke
    21:20-38

29 2 Sam. 21–22; Luke 22:1-30

30 2 Sam. 23–24; Luke 22:31-53

MAY

1   1 Kings 1–2; Luke 22:54-71

2   1 Kings 3–5; Luke 23:1-26

3   1 Kings 6–7; Luke 23:27-38

4   1 Kings 8–9; Luke 23:39-56

5   1 Kings 10–11; Luke 24:1-35

6   1 Kings 12–13; Luke
    24:36-53

7   1 Kings 14–15; John 1:1-28

8   1 Kings 16–18; John 1:29-51

9   1 Kings 19–20; John 2

10 1 Kings 21–22; John 3:1-21

11 2 Kings 1–3; John 3:22-36

12 2 Kings 4–5; John 4:1-30

13 2 Kings 6–8; John 4:31-54

14 2 Kings 9–11; John 5:1-24

15 2 Kings 12–14; John 5:25-47

16 2 Kings 15–17; John 6:1-21

17 2 Kings 18–19; John 6:22-44

18 2 Kings 20–22; John 6:45-71

19 2 Kings 23–25; John 7:1-31

20 1 Chron. 1–2; John 7:32-53

21 1 Chron. 3–5; John 8:1-20

22 1 Chron. 6–7; John 8:21-36

23 1 Chron. 8–10; John 8:37-59

24 1 Chron. 11–13; John 9:1-23

25 1 Chron. 14–16; John
    9:24-41

26 1 Chron. 17–19; John
    10:1-21

27 1 Chron. 20–22; John
    10:22-42

28 1 Chron. 23–25; John
    11:1-17

29 1 Chron. 26–27; John
    11:18-46

30 1 Chron. 28–29; John
    11:47-57

31 2 Chron. 1–3; John 12:1-19

JUNE

1   2 Chron. 4–6; John 12:20-50

2   2 Chron. 7–9; John 13:1-17

3   2 Chron. 10–12; John
    13:18-38

4   2 Chron. 13–16; John 14

5   2 Chron. 17–19; John 15

6　2 Chron. 20–22; John 16:1-15

7　2 Chron. 23–25; John 16:16-33

8　2 Chron. 26–28; John 17

9　2 Chron. 29–31; John 18:1-23

10　2 Chron. 32–33; John 18:24-40

11　2 Chron. 34–36; John 19:1-22

12　Ezra 1–2; John 19:23-42

13　Ezra 3–5; John 20

14　Ezra 6–8; John 21

15　Ezra 9–10; Acts 1

16　Neh. 1–3; Acts 2:1-13

17　Neh. 4–6; Acts 2:14-47

18　Neh. 7–8; Acts 3

19　Neh. 9–11; Acts 4:1-22

20　Neh. 12–13; Acts 4:23-37

21　Esth. 1–3; Acts 5:1-16

22　Esth. 4–6; Acts 5:17-42

23　Esth. 7–10; Acts 6

24　Job 1–3; Acts 7:1-19

25　Job 4–6; Acts 7:20-43

26　Job 7–9; Acts 7:44-60

27　Job 10–12; Acts 8:1-25

28　Job 13–15; Acts 8:26-40

29　Job 16–18; Acts 9:1-22

30　Job 19–20; Acts 9:23-43

JULY

1　Job 21–22; Acts 10:1-23

2　Job 23–25; Acts 10:24-48

3　Job 26–28; Acts 11

4　Job 29–30; Acts 12

5　Job 31–32; Acts 13:1-23

6　Job 33–34; Acts 13:24-52

7　Job 35–37; Acts 14

8　Job 38–39; Acts 15:1-21

9　Job 40–42; Acts 15:22-41

10　Ps. 1–3; Acts 16:1-15

11　Ps. 4–6; Acts 16:16-40

12　Ps. 7–9; Acts 17:1-15

13　Ps. 10–12; Acts 17:16-34

14　Ps. 13–16; Acts 18

15　Ps. 17–18; Acts 19:1-20

16　Ps. 19–21; Acts 19:21-41

17　Ps. 22–24; Acts 20:1-16

18　Ps. 25–27; Acts 20:17-38

19　Ps. 28–30; Acts 21:1-14

20　Ps. 31–33; Acts 21:15-40

21　Ps. 34–35; Acts 22

22　Ps. 36–37; Acts 23:1-11

23　Ps. 38–40; Acts 23:12-35

24　Ps. 41–43; Acts 24

25　Ps. 44–46; Acts 25

26　Ps. 47–49; Acts 26

27　Ps. 50–52; Acts 27:1-25

28　Ps. 53–55; Acts 27:26-44

29　Ps. 56–58; Acts 28:1-15

30 Ps. 59–61; Acts 28:16-31

31 Ps. 62–64; Rom. 1

AUGUST

1 Ps. 65–67; Rom. 2

2 Ps. 68–69; Rom. 3

3 Ps. 70–72; Rom. 4

4 Ps. 73–74; Rom. 5

5 Ps. 75–77; Rom. 6

6 Ps. 78; Rom. 7

7 Ps. 79–81; Rom. 8:1-18

8 Ps. 82–84; Rom. 8:19-39

9 Ps. 85–87; Rom. 9

10 Ps. 88–89; Rom. 10

11 Ps. 90–92; Rom. 11:1-21

12 Ps. 93–95; Rom. 11:22-36

13 Ps. 96–98; Rom. 12

14 Ps. 99–102; Rom. 13

15 Ps. 103–104; Rom. 14

16 Ps. 105–106; Rom. 15:1-20

17 Ps. 107–108; Rom. 15:21-33

18 Ps. 109–111; Rom. 16

19 Ps. 112–115; 1 Cor. 1

20 Ps. 116–118; 1 Cor. 2

21 Ps. 119:1-48; 1 Cor. 3

22 Ps. 119:49-104; 1 Cor. 4

23 Ps. 119:105-176; 1 Cor. 5

24 Ps. 120–123; 1 Cor. 6

25 Ps. 124–127; 1 Cor. 7:1-24

26 Ps. 128–131; 1 Cor. 7:25-40

27 Ps. 132–135; 1 Cor. 8

28 Ps. 136–138; 1 Cor. 9

29 Ps. 139–141; 1 Cor. 10:1-13

30 Ps. 142–144; 1 Cor. 10:14-33

31 Ps. 145–147; 1 Cor. 11:1-15

SEPTEMBER

1 Ps. 148–150; 1 Cor. 11:16-34

2 Prov. 1–2; 1 Cor. 12

3 Prov. 3–4; 1 Cor. 13

4 Prov. 5–6; 1 Cor. 14:1-20

5 Prov. 7–8; 1 Cor. 14:21-40

6 Prov. 9–10; 1 Cor. 15:1-32

7 Prov. 11–12; 1 Cor. 15:33-58

8 Prov. 13–14; 1 Cor. 16

9 Prov. 15–16; 2 Cor. 1

10 Prov. 17–18; 2 Cor. 2

11 Prov. 19–20; 2 Cor. 3

12 Prov. 21–22; 2 Cor. 4

13 Prov. 23–24; 2 Cor. 5

14 Prov. 25–27; 2 Cor. 6

15 Prov. 28–29; 2 Cor. 7

16 Prov. 30–31; 2 Cor. 8

17 Eccl. 1–3; 2 Cor. 9

18 Eccl. 4–6; 2 Cor. 10

19 Eccl. 7–9; 2 Cor. 11:1-15

OCTOBER

NOVEMBER

14 Ezek. 7–9; Heb. 10:24-39
15 Ezek. 10–12; Heb. 11:1-19
16 Ezek. 13–15; Heb. 11:20-40
17 Ezek. 16; Heb. 12
18 Ezek. 17–19; Heb. 13
19 Ezek. 20–21; James 1
20 Ezek. 22–23; James 2
21 Ezek. 24–26; James 3
22 Ezek. 27–28; James 4
23 Ezek. 29–31; James 5
24 Ezek. 32–33; 1 Pet. 1
25 Ezek. 34–35; 1 Pet. 2
26 Ezek. 36–37; 1 Pet. 3
27 Ezek. 38–39; 1 Pet. 4
28 Ezek. 40; 1 Pet. 5
29 Ezek. 41–42; 2 Pet. 1
30 Ezek. 43–44; 2 Pet. 2

DECEMBER

1 Ezek. 45–46; 2 Pet. 3
2 Ezek. 47–48; 1 John 1
3 Dan. 1–2; 1 John 2
4 Dan. 3–4; 1 John 3
5 Dan. 5–6; 1 John 4
6 Dan. 7–8; 1 John 5

7 Dan. 9–10; 2 John
8 Dan. 11–12; 3 John
9 Hos. 1–4; Jude
10 Hos. 5–8; Rev. 1
11 Hos. 9–11; Rev. 2
12 Hos. 12–14; Rev. 3
13 Joel; Rev. 4
14 Amos 1–3; Rev. 5
15 Amos 4–6; Rev. 6
16 Amos 7–9; Rev. 7
17 Obad.; Rev. 8
18 Jon.; Rev. 9
19 Mic. 1–3; Rev. 10
20 Mic. 4–5; Rev. 11
21 Mic. 6–7; Rev. 12
22 Nah.; Rev. 13
23 Hab.; Rev. 14
24 Zeph.; Rev. 15
25 Hag.; Rev. 16
26 Zech. 1–3; Rev. 17
27 Zech. 4–6; Rev. 18
28 Zech. 7–9; Rev. 19
29 Zech. 10–12; Rev. 20
30 Zech. 13–14; Rev. 21
31 Mal.; Rev. 22

Scriptures on the Power of Our Words

1. "Death and life are in the power of the tongue..."—Proverbs 18:21

   COMMENT: By our own tongue, the Bible says we have the power to speak death or life over ourselves and our circumstances, our children, finances, or a loved one who is sick. Notice how the emphasis in this verse is not on the power of death and life, but the power of the *tongue*.

2. "Words are powerful; take them seriously. Words can be your salvation. Words can be your damnation."—Matthew 12:36–37 MSG

    COMMENT: Jesus corroborates the previous verse, telling us that our words have the power to "make us or break us."

3. "For assuredly, I say to you, whoever says to this mountain, 'Be removed and be cast into the sea,' and does not doubt in his heart, but believes that those things he says will come to pass, he will have whatever he says."— Mark 11:23

    COMMENT: Jesus didn't tell us here to just pray about the mountain, but *speak to* the mountain. This applies to any "mountain" in our life, whether it's an illness, financial problem, etc. He goes on to say that if we don't doubt in our heart, we will have *whatever* things we say. If we speak negatively, we'll get negative results; if we speak positively, we'll get positive results.

4. "Indeed, we put bits in horses' mouths that they may obey us, and we turn their whole body. Look also at ships: although they are so large and are driven by fierce winds, they are turned by a very small rudder wherever the pilot desires. Even so the tongue is a little member and boasts great things."—James 3:3–5

COMMENT: This verse makes it so clear that our tongue determines the whole direction of our life—just like the bit in a horse's mouth or the rudder of a ship determines its direction.

5. "...he who has My word, let him speak My word faithfully.... 'Is not My word like a fire?' says the LORD, 'and like a hammer that breaks the rock in pieces?'"—Jeremiah 23:28–29

6. "A man will be satisfied with good by the fruit of his mouth..."—Proverbs 12:14

COMMENT: This amazing verse tells us so clearly how to be satisfied with good: by the fruit (words) of our mouth. If we want to be satisfied with good, we have to speak words of faith and victory out of our mouth at all times.

7. "And they [the saints] overcame him [the devil, the accuser of the brethren] by the blood of the Lamb and by the word of their testimony..."—Revelation 12:11

COMMENT: This verse doesn't say we overcome the devil with the *thought* of our testimony, but the *word* of our testimony. Our "testimony" is what God's Word says about us. Everything else is either a lie from the enemy or wrong thinking on our part. The word of your testimony has to be spoken, like Jesus did when He was tempted by the devil in the wilderness. He told the devil three times, "It is written..." in Matthew 4:4–10. He quoted Scripture to him and declared what the Word of God said about Him, and the devil eventually left Him (Matthew 4:11).

8. "He who guards his mouth keeps his life, but he who opens wide his lips shall have destruction."—Proverbs 13:3

9. "Whoever guards his mouth and tongue keeps his soul from troubles."—Proverbs 21:23

10. "You are snared by the words of your mouth..."—Proverbs 6:2

Daily Positive Confessions

"[You] will have whatever [you] say."
MARK 11:23

Many times, the way we start the day determines what kind of day we're going to have. That's why it's so important that we get our mind going in the right direction first thing in the morning. And that's why the enemy loves to attack our mind the minute we wake up. Use these positive confessions to speak out loud every morning to get your mind and mouth in agreement with God and programmed for victory. Memorize as many as you can, and meditate on them and speak them over yourself throughout the day. The thoughts you think and words you speak today will determine your tomorrow.

- I am blessed.
- I am forgiven and redeemed.
- I am loved, accepted, and approved.
- I am free—free from sickness, poverty, lack, and every kind of bondage or stronghold.
- I am secure and confident.
- I am wise, intelligent, and creative.
- I am focused and disciplined.
- I am successful.
- I am talented.
- I am anointed.
- I am prosperous.
- I am healthy.
- I am full of vim, vigor, vitality, energy, and strength.
- I am God's masterpiece, created in His image and likeness.
- I am a person of divine purpose and destiny.
- I am a child of the Most High God.
- In all things I am more than a conqueror (Romans 8:37).

- I can do all things through Christ who strengthens me (Philippians 4:13).
- God always causes me to triumph in Christ Jesus (2 Corinthians 2:14).
- God's favor surrounds me like a shield (Psalm 5:12).
- God's goodness and mercy follow me all the days of my life (Psalm 23:6).
- God has plans to prosper me, to give me a hope and a future (Jeremiah 29:11).
- My path is like the shining sun, shining brighter and brighter until the full day (Proverbs 4:18).
- God is perfecting everything that concerns me (Psalm 138:8).

Prayer of Salvation

If you have never formally asked Jesus to be your Lord and Savior, or maybe you've grown cold toward the Lord and need to rededicate your life, I invite you to take a minute and do that now. The Bible says *today* is the day of salvation because tomorrow is not guaranteed. You may not have the opportunity to make this decision later, so don't put it off. Pray this simple prayer and ask Jesus into your heart:

> *Lord Jesus, I repent of all my sins. I ask You to come into my heart and wash me clean. I make You my Lord and Savior. Thank You, Jesus, for saving me and making me a part of the family of God. Help me to follow You all of my days. In Jesus' name, Amen.*

If you prayed that simple prayer, the Bible says you were "born again." That just means you have a brand-new life in Christ. You are no longer separated from God in sin. Jesus paid the price for all your sins—past, present, and future—so you could be in the family of God. The Bible also says you are a new creation in Christ. You may not feel any different at first, but as you continue walking with Christ, you will gradually become more like Him.

Next Steps

To help you grow in your walk with the Lord,
I encourage you to:

1. Get into a good Bible-teaching church.
2. Don't spend time with friends who are going to pull you away from your walk with the Lord. Instead, invite them to come to church with you.
3. Talk to God daily through prayer. You don't need to pray fancy prayers, just be yourself and talk to God like a loving Father.
4. Read your Bible daily to gain a deeper understanding of God and the Christian life.

STAY**CONNECTED**
BE**BLESSED.**

From thoughtful articles to powerful blogs, podcasts and more, JoelOsteen.com is full of inspirations that will give you encouragement and confidence in your daily life.

AVAILABLE ON JOELOSTEEN.COM

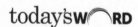

This daily devotional from Joel and Victoria will help you grow in your relationship with the Lord and equip you to be everything God intends you to be.

 **Joel Osteen STREAMING**

Miss a broadcast? Watch Joel Osteen on demand, and see Joel LIVE on Sundays.

 **Joel Osteen PODCAST**

The podcast is a great way to listen to Joel where you want, when you want.

CONNECT WITH US

PUT JOEL IN YOUR POCKET

Join our community of believers on your favorite social network.

Get the inspiration and encouragement of Joel Osteen on your iPhone, iPad or Android device! Our app puts Joel's messages, devotions and more at your fingertips.

Thanks for helping us make a difference in the lives of millions around the world.